Power Writing

From Paragraph to Essay

Nicole van Woudenberg

Smart Teacher:
Teacher Career & Retirement Planning

First Edition September 2024

Published by 85 After School Media. Cover design by 85 After School Media.

85afterschool@gmail.com

ISBN: 978-1-0688524-3-5 ebook

ISBN: 978-1-0688524-2-8 book

Designed in Canada.

Author information for Nicole van Woudenberg: 85afterschool@gmail.com

Table of Contents

Preface

I love teaching. Maybe not so much on the most challenging of days but overall I know I chose the right career for me. Having taught for over twenty-five years students as young as four right through adults, I have seen my fair share of reluctant writers. And I know you have heard more often than you care to count "I don't know what to write about", followed by a huff, sagging shoulders and perhaps disruptive behaviour. Or when you ask your students to write about a topic and they say, "How long does it have to be?" as if you are asking them to move a mountain. It's frustrating. You think you have taught them to write a simple paragraph and they still only write a half-coherent sentence or two. I get it.

I tried everything: the hamburger model, free-write, bite-size writing, persuasive map, T-table, sequence chart... to name but a few. I don't have an undergrad degree in English nor am I a Literacy specialist so I started digging deeper into what strategies actually get results for all students, not only those gifted in language arts. With my special education background, I quickly learned you need to really break things down, model, practise and practise some more. Where a student without any learning issues may require, for example, twenty trials to build neurological pathways to learn a new skill or concept, students with learning differences may require four times as many trials, if not more. As teachers we know we have a spectrum of learners and we use a variety of strategies to try to convey a new skill or concept. However, my smorgasbord of strategies mentioned earlier really didn't produce any consistent written output.

Frustrated and about to give up, I came across the *Power Writing* process. Digging deeper into what it entails from several sources, I learned that the most important part is the consistency of executing the process and using the graphic organizer. I tried it with my Grade 7 class, an inclusive group of students. I noticed that students, even with ADHD, ASD or learning disabilities were able to independently write a paragraph. More importantly, they weren't asking "how long does it have to be?" nor saying "I don't know what to write about". I was cautiously optimistic. As the weeks went on and I consistently taught the process, I noticed the students were starting to organize their thoughts using *Power Writing* in various subjects. I started deliberately assigning students to communicate what they learned in Math, Science, Social Studies even Health Studies using the *Power Writing* process. It was working.

Still skeptical, especially when these types of suggestions come from over-enthusiastic workshop facilitators who haven't actually tried it with students themselves, I decided to seek funding to undertake a project with other teachers. I was able to work with several elementary and middle-school teachers, including two in the role of special education resource. To our great delight, after months of using the process in our classrooms, we had samples from Kindergarten through Grade 8 where even the most reluctant writers were producing paragraphs. As a group of practising teachers we knew we had something that needed to be shared with others.

Through teacher moderation, we created a checklist and rubric to meet the curriculum standards. We collected samples from Kindergarten through Grade 8 and collectively determined the corresponding mark. The samples were meant to assist other teachers to have a benchmark of what the work could look like. We even identified work produced by students who had learning differences, for the purpose of demonstrating that this process works for all students. Mind you, the samples ranged in levels as not everyone was performing at the highest level. However, students became much more independent, accountable and most importantly, didn't leave the page blank!

This experience motivated me to write this book. After all, a good idea needs to be shared. If you ever have an opportunity as a practising classroom teacher to work with colleagues, specifically to participate in teacher-moderation, jump on it. For me it was such a rewarding learning experience that it reenergized my teaching career. Hopefully in reading this book, you too will find the great success I have with my students when I teach them the *Power Writing* process.

Introduction

"Writing is a craft before it is an art; writing may appear magic, but it is our responsibility to take our students backstage to watch the pigeons being tucked up in the magician's sleeve."

- Donald Murray

As educators, we are challenged to demystify the writing process for our students. This has long been an often, elusive goal for classroom teachers as some methods seemed to reveal genius in some students, while others floundered under the same instruction. Enabling our students to express their ideas, opinions, stories and reflections in written form is a weighty responsibility. Our classrooms are comprised of students with diverse skillsets, abilities and learning styles, and it has become apparent that no single writing program alone can satisfy the needs of our students.

Supported by research, it is the firm belief that excellent writing instruction includes ideas and practices from a variety of writing programs and resources. *The 3 Steps to Powerful Writing*, by Betty

Hamilton, and *Teach the Traits of Effective Writing*, by Shirley Poulton, promote the consistent use of a graphic organizer (effective visual strategy) and a methodical, step-by-step approach to effective paragraph writing. This method meets the needs of students who require an explicit, systematic approach to developing paragraphs that include a central theme and supporting details. By concurrently teaching the traits of writing, we can provide our students with opportunities to move from concrete to more abstract thinking.

No one program can meet the needs of all students as many have different learning styles. Differentiating instruction for the diverse populations within our classrooms is key to providing multiple entry points for success. We can provide structure and concrete methods for those who require it, while encouraging others to stretch their thinking and incorporate more sophisticated nuances of writing into their pieces. However, we have used the *Power Writing* process in our teaching and even the most reluctant of writers will produce well-structured paragraphs and then see themselves as capable.

If we truly believe that all children can succeed and become competent writers, then we must layer our teaching. At the foundation are the ideas born out of purposeful talk and fashioned into a writer's mainstay - a basic paragraph. From there the traits are artfully applied - ideas, voice, word choice, sentence fluency, conventions, presentation - until the piece is transformed into something uniquely their own. The *6 + 1 Traits of Writing*, by Ruth Culham, dives more deeply into these aspects of the written word. Although each of your students will reach a different level of competency, starting with the power writing approach will allow all students to reach a baseline level of success. As their self-confidence in their writing grows, they will experiment more and achieve greater levels of success. As educators, our goal is to reveal the secrets behind a well-constructed piece of writing, unlocking the doors to self-expression for our students.

Each child that we teach has the ability to communicate in various forums and formats. As educators we model, teach and guide students to become proficient communicators in speech, written, and visual formats. This book is meant as a resource for teachers, students and homeschoolers. More importantly it is about choosing teaching strategies that will enable students at any age to express thoughts, ideas, opinions and feelings.

Structure of the Book

You have made a wise choice with this book as it will not only provide you with the framework of how to teach students as young as kindergarteners how to formulate and organize their ideas, you'll be able to see age-appropriate samples for elementary and middle-schoolers. Those samples, written by real students, come with an assessment and explanation of the graded result. More importantly, it provides the next steps to help the student progress to a more advanced level. The book includes ready-to-use rubrics for your classroom, no matter what subject you teach. You can then use those rubrics as a starting point to tailor them to your specific subject or topic of study.

The Framework & Graphic Organizer

It is important for you to internalize the *Power Writing* structure. There are strategies to teach your students before they begin to use the graphic organizer to write their first paragraph. Be sure to familiarize yourself with the building blocks for the most successful results with your group of students. Just like any concept you teach, there will be a spectrum of learners with a bellcurve of results. However, eventually, with consistency, you'll move that bellcurve to lean towards the right instead of remaining in the middle. The graphic organizer is the tool that helps jumpstart the writing process. Students should not take shortcuts. Be sure to always model the importance of the graphic organizer. If you follow the simple steps as described, you will see that even the most reluctant of writers is able to produce a coherent paragraph.

About the Samples

All the samples included in this book are written by real students. We use samples, not exemplars, as they are meant to provide an example of what students *may* produce not what they *should* produce if you were to replicate the topic or activity. Some of the original written text may not be legible (for example, creative spelling by kindergarteners) so the handwritten text has been reproduced in typed-form. The creative spelling may remain in the transposed text but may have a clarification in brackets. Again, it is a sample to help you grasp what a kindergartener, elementary or middle-schooler is capable of producing at various levels.

About the Rubrics

In North America there is a common grading system of letter grades and percentage marks. Except for the *Kindergarten Checklist*, the assessments of the samples in this book follow a levelling system that is easily translated to a letter grade or percentage. Note that a Level 1 is defined as the student demonstrating limited understanding of the knowledge, skill or application described in the category. It is still a pass but it is translated to a D letter-grade or within the range of 50 - 59 percent. Perhaps that range is not a passing level in your jurisdiction so adjust your grading accordingly. Level 2 performance indicates that the student is demonstrating some of the knowledge, skill or application of the required category or approaching what you would expect for the grade level or curriculum expectation. This would translate into a C letter-grade or between 60 - 69 percentage mark. It follows then that Level 3 congratulates the student on meeting the expectation of the category. They have demonstrated the knowledge, skill or application of what is expected but not beyond. It would translate into a B letter-grade or within the 70s for a percentage mark. Now, you may be thinking, "But if they've done exactly what they were asked to do, why not give them an A?". Great question! We always provide students with a challenge to go beyond what is expected so that there is opportunity to push themselves further. We can only do this if we provide the students with the rubric or expectations of what each level looks-like at the beginning of the assignment. For this reason, Level 4 will always have the extended, go one-step further criteria so that students have the opportunity to demonstrate their knowledge, skill or application at a higher flevel. This is the A letter-grade or 80-100 percentage mark. Of course, if you have curriculum guidelines that require you to assess and evaluate in a more traditional format, you can still use the content of the rubrics as the levels can easily be translated to fit your requirements.

The traditional structure of a rubric has the criteria listed on the left and then the next column typically begins with the lowest level. However, since we really want our students to strive to be the best they can be, we have reversed and started with the highest level and placed the lowest to the far right. Again, if this is not permitted in your practice (which I don't understand why you wouldn't be allowed to psychologically set your students up for success), you can easily change the rubric to reflect the traditional format.

Summary

Artificial Intelligence has both positive and negative consequences for students who need to learn how to write. If we think about the idea-generating stage, the brainstorming, we know that AI can do that and more. However, knowing that many of us use nonfiction writing in most of our daily work, we also know that focus, precision and directness is the key to communicating clearly. AI does not own your voice. Neither is it able to get the nuances your personal experiences in your specific work location have afforded you. Hence, students still need to be able to learn how to write in a consistent manner, with or without AI tools. They need to be able to think, generate, produce or check that the written paragraph is expressing a main idea with supporting ideas, tailored for their specific situation. *Power Writing* is definitely a skill that once learned will be used throughout one's life, with or without artificial intelligence tools.

Part 1

The Power Writing Process

CHAPTER ONE

Teaching Power Writing to K-8 Students

This chapter will help you become familiar with the *Power Writing* process. It describes all the important elements that students will need to learn: brainstorming, selecting worthy ideas, using the graphic organizer, choosing appropriate transition words and writing simple to complex sentences. Learning these skills will help students become more confident in following the structured process. The next chapter will walk you through a tangible example of how to teach it in eight, easy steps. For now, let's begin with the simplest form of *Power Writing* that you will teach your students no matter if they are in kindergarten or middle school.

The Powers of Power Writing

There are three powers. The process assigns numerical power to words, phrases, sentences and paragraphs:

- **Power 1**: Main idea (it includes the topic and last sentence in a paragraph)
- **Power 2**: Major detail related back to main idea (supporting details)
- **Power 3**: Minor detail (an elaboration of a Power 2)

When first introducing *Power Writing*, you only deal with Power 1 and Power 2. This will have students construct a topic/opening sentence (Power 1), a closing sentence (Power 1) and then for each of the three major details of the topic (Power 2) write a simple sentence. Thus, such a paragraph would have five sentences in total (topic, major detail, major detail, major detail and, closing sentence). The pattern would be 1-2-2-2-1.

As students become more proficient in writing a five-paragraph sentence, you would introduce to them Power 3, the minor detail that elaborates on the associated Power 2 major detail. The paragraph would therefore grow from five sentences to eight sentences: topic sentence, closing sentence (Power 1), three major detail sentences (Power 2) and three corresponding minor detail (Power 3) associated with each of the three major details. The pattern would be 1-2-3-2-3-2-3-1.

You can see how the above paragraph structure is mechanical and as students become confident in applying the formula we want them to add their creativity or *voice* to their writing. **Power Zero** is introductory, explanatory material leading to the main idea. It is the sentence that grabs the attention of the reader just before the first power. The pattern would be 0-1-2-3-2-3-2-3-1. You can also teach

Power Zero to students who are writing five-sentence paragraphs with the 0-1-2-2-2-1 pattern.

Once students have mastered writing a paragraph you can introduce to middle-schoolers the five-paragraph essay structure. The five-paragraph essay structure has the same pattern where the introductory paragraph and the closing paragraph is considered your Power 1 and the three paragraphs in between are your Power 2. Within the body of the essay (the three, Power 2 paragraphs), the student would follow the paragraph pattern of 0-1-2-2-2-1 or 0-1-2-3-2-3-2-3-1 where Power Zero may or may not be necessary or useful. If it's difficult for you to visualize it at this point, don't worry, the samples later on in the book will help bring it to life.

Considerations

It is important to teach students how to brainstorm, produce ideas and scrutinize what ideas are well-linked or connected to the topic. Modelling writing in your classroom to show how to elaborate on ideas (from major, Power 2, to minor, Power 3) is very important. You will want to do a lot of modelling for revision and editing as well. Making it a group (or small-group) direct lesson helps students practise - and they need a lot of practise! When first introducing the powers of power writing, teach students to indent, the visual is powerful in and of itself. Also teach them never to use the word "because" or "so" when teaching them the 1-2-2-2-1 pattern. Those two words tend to take away Power 3 elaboration which you will be teaching after they have mastered the 1-2-2-2-1 pattern. Sometimes "and" also creates a problem as it also tends to elaborate which, is a Power 3.

Never underestimate the importance of modelling. Encourage revision of paragraphs already written which can be done whole-class or in a small group with partners. Remember, you can use power writing in any subject. I often use it in my unit assessment where the student writes a power paragraph explaining, for example, how they reached an answer in a math word-problem or how they would design a science experiment to test a theory that we have been discussing in class. I have assigned students to explain the emotions evoked by listening to two completely different genres of music. A very effective way for students to practise demonstrating their knowledge, understanding and application on an assessment is with TTQA (turn-the-question-around). Once students have internalized the structure, they spend much more time on the brainstorming requirement than on just writing random ideas. And there's nothing wrong with incorporating the power of AI when modelling brainstorming. What is important though is being able to critically select the most relevant ideas. Hence, I cannot emphasize enough the power of modelling brainstorming, scrutinizing and selecting ideas and then, modelling the writing process, editing, revising and sharing their written work.

When assessing or evaluating the student's work, mark each sentence to ensure it is accurate and complete. Remember when first teaching the 1-2-2-2-1 pattern, be very strict about not using "because" or "so". You will probably see later on when students become proficient with sentence structure and flow that "because" and "so" will work in the 1-2-3-2-3-2-3-1 pattern. From my experience, it is difficult to move students to the more advance stage if they have not been told to avoid “because” or “so” when first learning *Power Writing*.

In the beginning, students also do better when you bring errors to their attention immediately while they are engaged in the writing process. It’s good practice to circulate amongst your students. Lots of practise will help students improve. They don’t have to start a new piece each time, they can work on rough drafts that are kept in their portfolio and revisit to practise.

Brainstorming

Do you have effective strategies to help your students brainstorm ideas long before they even pick up a pencil, put fingers on a keyboard or dictate their writing to a device? Use these strategies to help them feel successful when you ask them to write about a specific topic. Some of my favourite ways to help students come up with on-topic ideas are think-pair-share, K-W-L, whole-class brainstorm, pre-read or, video-intro for minds-on, to name but a few. Not sure what they are? See Appendix 1 at the end of the book for a brief explanation of each. Again, you can use AI to help generate ideas but don’t make it the default. Students need to use their own personal knowledge and experience to help them critically choose ideas related to the topic.

Graphic Organizer

Once students have brainstormed about a certain topic and the main points that connect best to the topic have been identified, you will model how to use the graphic organizer. The graphic organizer is a must and students should not skip using it consistently. It is a simple backwards "C" with three arms extending from the vertical line. The graphic organizer will have Power 1 labeled at the top and bottom horizontal lines. Power 2 will be labeled on the three arm extensions. On the inside of the graphic organizer it is important that you write the three transition words that students will use consistently when they first begin to use the *Power Writing* process. As you model, write "First, Second, Third," on the inside of the graphic organizer adjacent to the Power 2 lines. Only then are you ready to add the topic Power 1 words and the major details, Power 2 words (and minor details, Power 3, when you progress to the advanced pattern). It is important to keep it to words or brief phrases (three-word phrases at most) so that students don't start writing sentences in their graphic organizer, that's not the idea.

Graphic Organizer Using 1-2-2-2-1 Pattern

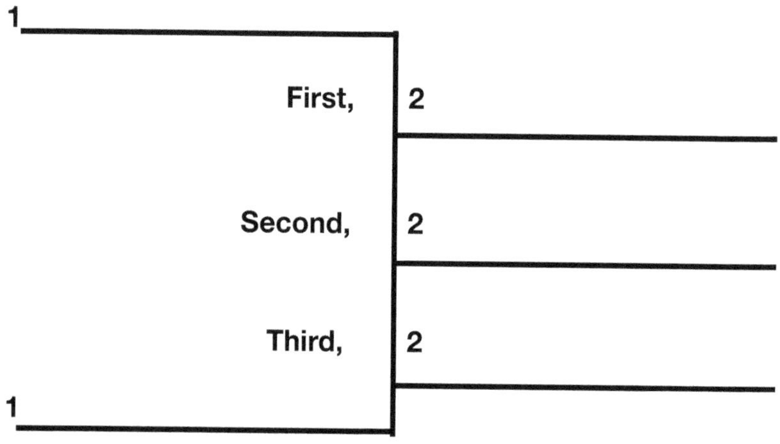

Graphic Organizer Using 1-2-3-2-3-2-3-1 Pattern

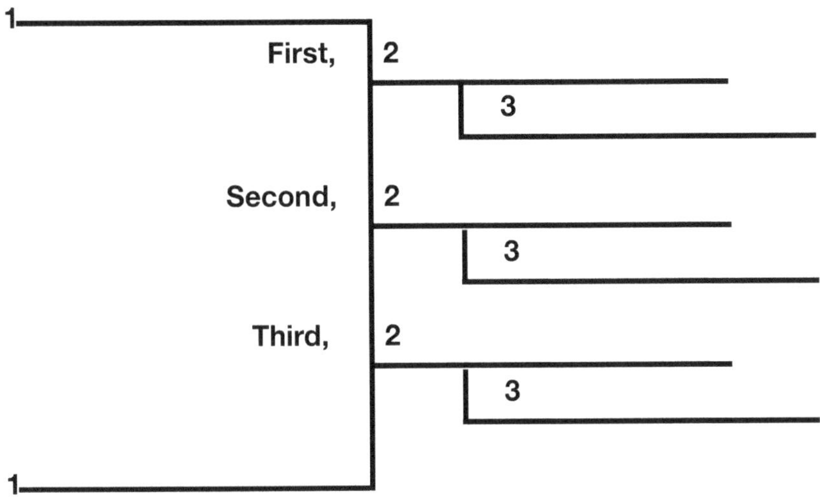

Graphic Organizer Pattern, Using Power Zero

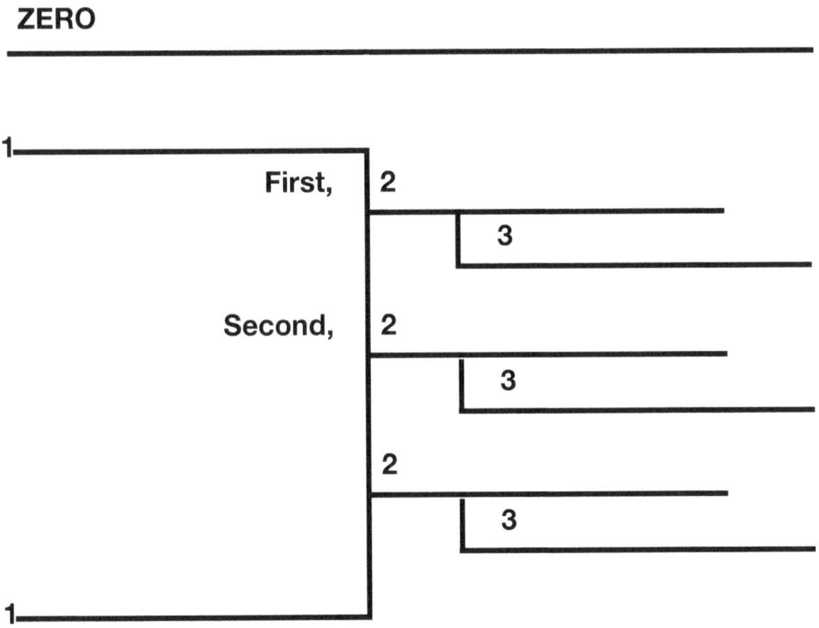

ZERO

1

First,

2

3

Second,

2

3

2

3

1

Transition Words

To signal change from one idea to the next writers use transition words to help with flow. Transition words are used in oral language as well to ensure the listener can follow the speaker's train of thought. Since strong oral language skills help develop written skills as well, it is good to have students orally rehearse their thoughts and ideas using transition words as well. Here is a basic list of transition words that are helpful when formulating a power paragraph. Although we model with "First, Second, Third," when teaching power writing, eventually we want to expand our students' vocabulary and provide a wide range of transition words.

Transition Words

First (Firstly)	Second (Secondly)	Third (Thirdly)
To begin with	Also	In conclusion
One one hand	Besides	Finally
To start	Next	As a result
One way	Then	In summary

For a more extensive list, see Appendix 2.

Sentence Variety

It's important to model sentence variety as students mature. The younger students will write simple sentences as they mirror what they hear and see in books, conversations and what adults model. Simple sentences will form into more complex sentences with increasing vocabulary. Introducing students to interesting adjectives (instead of always using “nice”) and exciting verbs (rather than always using “said”) will help with developing their sentence structure. Many examples are provided in *The 3 Steps of Powerful Writing*, by Betty Hamilton. It’s helpful to have charts in your classroom that students can reference when they are looking for alternative adjectives or verbs to spice up their writing. A list of interesting adjectives and exciting verbs can be found in Appendix 3 to help you get started.

Summary

The core elements of *Power Writing* include brainstorming, understanding the Powers, using the graphic organizer and having a list of transition words to help students write a variety of sentences. Now that you understand the process, we will venture into how to break down and teach the essential steps to your students. The next chapter will show you how to use the graphic organizer and present you with sample paragraphs that you can use in your own classroom as a starting point.

CHAPTER TWO

The Eight-Step Process

These easy to follow steps will help you start internalizing how to teach *Power Writing* to your students. Eventually once you know the steps inside-out, you will easily tailor it to fit into your own teaching style.

Step 1: Brainstorming

In my first lesson to introduce *Power Writing* to my students I usually choose a topic familiar to them to encourage maximum participation. Gathering the students, I tell them we are going to work together to write a paragraph about our favourite snacks. I write or type "Snacks" in the middle of my white board so students know we are going to brainstorm. Then I tell them we are going to "Think, Pair, Share". I may say, "Now it's time to think to yourself for one minute about all the yummy things you love to eat when you feel like having a snack. Remember, this is the time to think to yourself". I want students to be engaged and have ownership when they later turn to a partner to discuss their initial ideas.

After that minute of independent thinking, I say “Ok, turn to your elbow partner and share the ideas that you thought of. See how many snacks are the same as your partner's.” I give them a couple of minutes to discuss and share with their partner. A pre-established signal has them finish their chat and focus as a group back to the front. Then I start asking the students to share with the class their ideas. The “Think, Pair, Share” ensures that even a student who has difficulty thinking of anything, now has at least a couple of ideas from a partner. This allows them to participate with the entire class. When brainstorming, there are no bad ideas but, students do know that eventually the most relevant ideas will become obvious. Depending on the age of the students, I either choose (for the younger group) three main ideas or have a democratic vote (for the older students), always signalling I will have a veto if the idea really isn't related.

An example brainstorm of favourite snacks resulted in the following, with the three most relevant ideas circled.

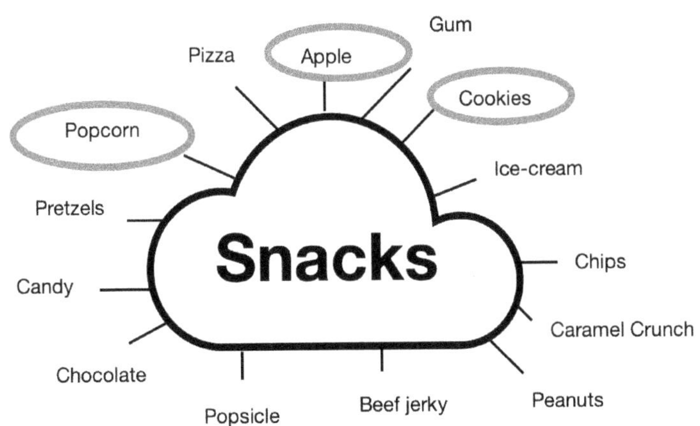

Step 2: Graphic Organizer

Now that we've brainstormed and selected the most relevant ideas related to our topic of favourite snacks, it is time to demonstrate how we take those ideas and organize them. We are using the 1-2-2-2-1 pattern in this example:

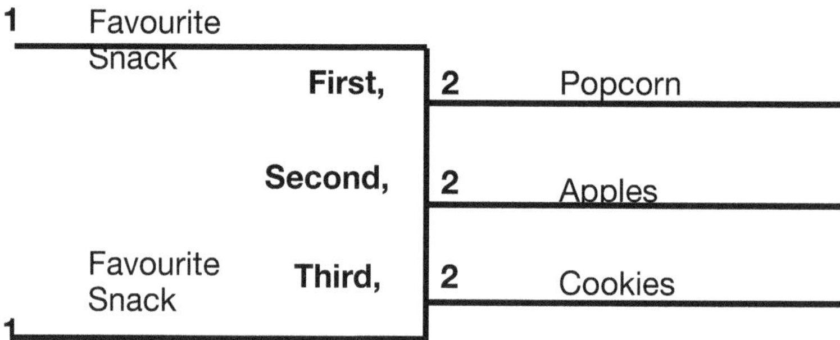

Students should complete the graphic organizer on the top-half of their page so they can do their rough draft below. It will be easier for reference if their graphic organizer is visible while writing. Once students become more familiar with how to use the graphic organizer as a tool, they can draw it themselves on the top corner of the page or pull up an electronic version and have two screens open to help them draft their written work.

Step 3: Power 1 - Opening and Closing Sentences

Now that the graphic organizer is complete, it is time to model for the students the topic and closing sentences. Note that in this book we use topic- or opening-sentence to mean the same thing. With younger students you may wish to stick the former. Writing the closing (or concluding) sentence at the beginning may seem out of order but because it is a Power 1, the idea is related and really it is a reformulation of the topic sentence. I tell the students that the topic and closing sentences are direct and general. In the example above, the topic is "favourite snacks" and I know I have three that I will talk about. I have the students read my example before they think of a sentence to share with the class. Remember we also coach the students not to use the words "because" or "so" in their sentence to avoid adding detail that is another power. Here are some examples of opening and closing sentences.

Topic/Opening Sentences

For kindergarten:
"I have three favourite snacks."

For elementary:
"There are three snacks I really like to eat."

For middle-school:
"When I want some snacks to eat, I always look for at least three."

Then reword it for the closing sentence.

Closing/Concluding Sentences

For kindergarten:
"Those are my three favourite snacks."

For elementary:

"I like many snacks, but popcorn, apples, and cookies are my favourite ones."

For middle-school:

"As you can see, popcorn, apples and cookies are a great choice if you want to eat a snack."

Step 4: Power 2 - Major Detail Sentences

Now that the topic and closing sentences have been written it is time to model for the students a simple sentence for each of the Power 2 points. Remind students that they should avoid "because" and "so" in their Power 2 sentences. Referencing the graphic organizer, there will be a sentence about popcorn, a sentence about apples and a sentence about cookies. Here is an example I would provide to the students before they brainstorm a variation. I also remind them to start the sentences with the transition words listed on the graphic organizer.

"First, I look for popcorn to pop."
"Second, I will check to see if we have apples."
"Third, I'm happy if I have some cookies."

By now you have constructed a 1-2-2-2-1 power paragraph and the students have participated in co-authorship even though you have modelled the construction of the sentences. Remember modelling and practising helps the students become more proficient and confident. The example below shows what a student's page may look like with the graphic organizer and their draft sentences. They would then write a first draft of the paragraph, reminding them to indent the topic sentence to signal the start of the paragraph. Remember, this is a sample and not an exemplar. It is what a student could produce not what a student should produce.

Step 5: Draft Paragraph - Student's Page

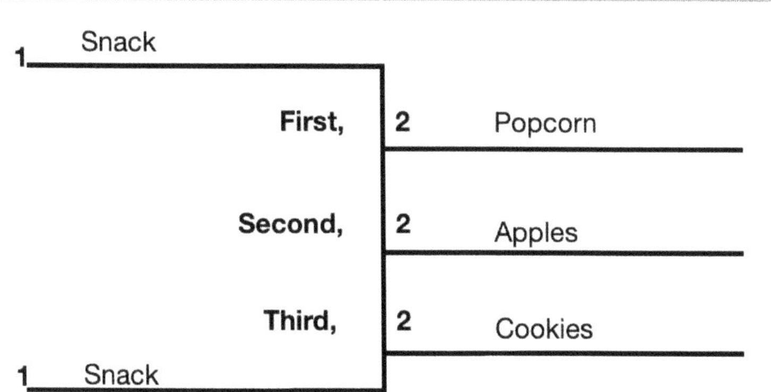

P1 When I want some snacks to eat, I always look for at least three.

P1 I like many snacks, but popcorn, apples, and cookies are my favourite ones.

P2 First, I look for popcorn to pop.

P2 Second, I will check to see if we have apples.

P2 Third, I'm happy if I have some cookies.

My Favourite Snacks

When I want some snacks to eat, I always look for at least three. First, I look for popcorn to pop. Second, I will check to see if we have any apples. Third, I'm happy if I have some cookies. I like many snacks, but popcorn, apples, and cookies are my favourite ones.

Step 6: Moving to 1-2-3-2-3-2-3-1 Pattern

You will know when students are ready to be introduced to the next level of power writing. It is important to explain to elementary and middle-school students that a Power 3 (minor detail) expands on the corresponding Power 2, major detail. When you have brainstormed three major details, ask students to think of a minor detail that can be tied to each of the three major details. For example, with our favourite snack popcorn, we might think about microwave popcorn. Maybe someone mentions their dad buys apples all the time. And perhaps most students think of chocolate chip cookies as the go-to snack. Let's see what a student's page could look like.

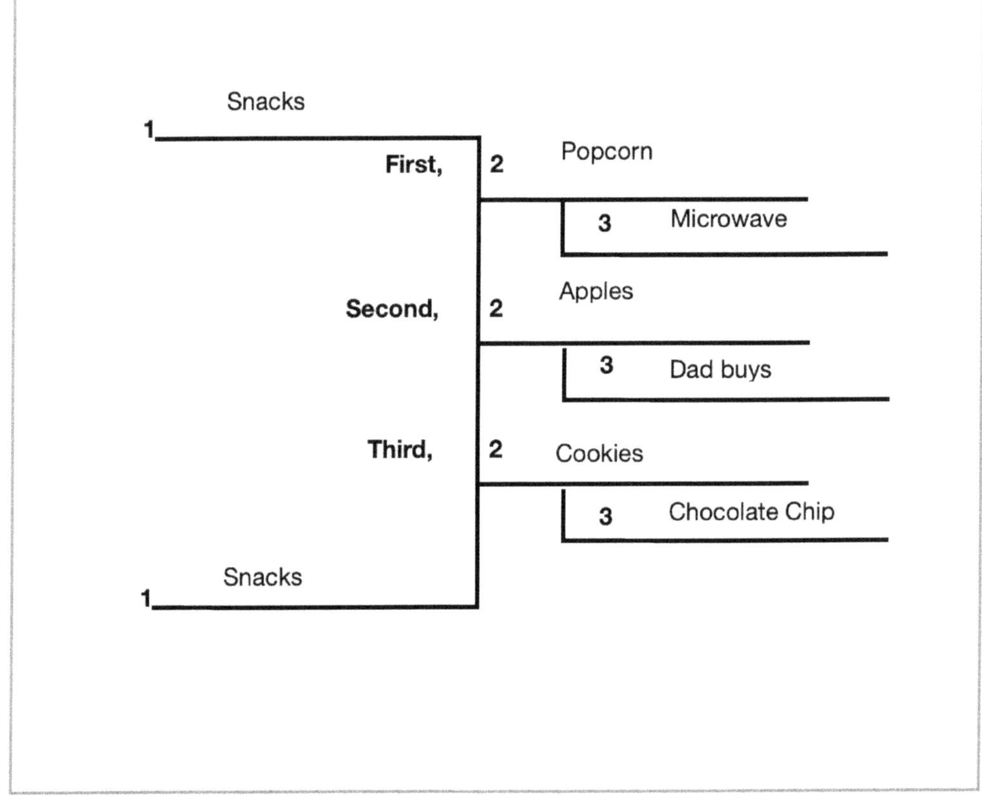

P1 When I want some snacks to eat, I always look for at least three.

P1 I like many snacks, but popcorn, apples, and cookies are my favourite ones.

P2 First, I look for popcorn to pop.

P3 If I find popcorn that I can put in the microwave, I have a fast snack.

P2 Second, I will check to see if we have apples.

P3 When I'm lucky, I find some that my dad bought at the supermarket.

P2 Third, I'm happy if I have some cookies.

P3 My favourite ones are chocolate chips.

My Favourite Snacks

When I want some snacks to eat, I always look for at least three. First, I look for popcorn to pop. If I find popcorn that I can put in the microwave, I have a fast snack. Second, I will check to see if we have any apples. When I'm lucky, I find some that my dad bought at the supermarket. Third, I'm happy if I find some cookies. My favourite ones are chocolate chip. I like many snacks, but popcorn, apples, and cookies are my favourite ones.

Step 7: Model Alternate Transition Words and Adding Power Zero

You can introduce the Power Zero before the 1-2-3-2-3-2-3-1 pattern, if you like. When students have really demonstrated their grasp for the core element of the 1-2-2-2-1 pattern, they can try to write an attention-grabbing hook. You know your students best and you will know when to introduce these concepts. See how different transition words can be dropped into the previous sample paragraph.

Change Transition Words

My Favourite Snacks

When I want some snacks to eat, I always look for at least three. **To begin with**, I look for popcorn to pop. If I find popcorn that I can put in the microwave, I have a fast snack. **Next**, I will check to see if we have any apples. When I'm lucky, I find some that my dad bought at the supermarket. **Finally**, I'm happy if I find some cookies. My favourite ones are chocolate chip. **To conclude,** I like many snacks, but popcorn, apples, and cookies are my favourite ones.

Adding Power Zero (0-1-2-3-2-3-2-3-1)

My Favourite Snacks

Pop, crunch, smack, these are a few of my favourite sounds! When I want some snacks to eat, I always look for at least three. To begin with, I look for popcorn to pop. If I find popcorn that I can put in the microwave, I have a fast snack. Next, I will check to see if we have any apples. When I'm lucky, I find some that my dad bought at the supermarket. Finally, I'm happy if I find some cookies. My favourite ones are chocolate chip. To conclude, I like many snacks, but popcorn, apples, and cookies are my favourite ones.

Step 8: Power Writing Integrated into Various Subjects

Power Writing works great for Math Journals

I solved the problem using the following three steps. First, I drew a picture of the swimming pool. Next, I labelled the length and the width of the pool. Finally, I calculated the area using the formula A = l x w. Therefore, the area of the swimming pool is 45 metres squared.

Power Writing to answer critical, thinking questions.

Try using TTQA - Turn The Question Around and answer it using the *Power Writing* process.

If the Bloodhound Gang had not used a code I think three terrible things might have happened. First of all, Vikki may not have been able to get help from the police. Next, if Vikki didn't get help she may have been seriously hurt or even killed by Billy the Blinker. Finally, Billy the Blinker might have gotten his revenge and killed Vikki's boss. I imagine those are the three terrible things that could have happened if they hadn't used the code.

Power Writing in Science, Social Studies, Geography and History

Lord Selkirk expected the settlers to make money three ways. First, he expected them to grow vegetables on the land that they were given to farm. Second, Selkirk expected them to provide beef and pork for the Western fur trade posh. Last, the settlers would have jobs with the Hudson's Bay Company. This ensured that the settlers would be able to sustain the settlement.

Summary

As you can see the steps are easy to follow and you will have success as long as you have your students practise often. It is so important to model, co-author and guide students as they progress from the simple pattern to the more advanced pattern. You can see how a simple, paragraph pattern can be expanded to write a five-paragraph essay. The opening paragraph would introduce the major ideas of each of the three body-paragraphs and the closing paragraph (the fifth paragraph) would be a summary of the three major points. It is important to be consistent in teaching the *Power Writing* process and not become lax in students' use of the graphic organizer, transition words or the order in which they construct their sentences. Follow the eight, easy steps and soon your students will become independent and precise writers.

Part 2

Samples, Rubrics & Evaluations

CHAPTER THREE

Kindergarten

You may think that kindergarteners are not able to produce written work except for random words with creative spelling. However, with modelling and practise, you will see young students use their oral language skills to follow the pattern in written form as well. Developmental stages of writing is outside of the scope of this book. However, we need to remember that young students write how they speak and so it is important to model back correct language structure. From experience, students as young as four are capable of grasping guided writing concepts, including the Power Writing process. The samples in this chapter provide various levels of written production from students aged four and five.

Kindergarten Graphic Organizer & Checklist

There are certain skills teachers model through guided writing. Young students will find generating ideas quite difficult as an independent task. Use a consistent graphic organizer so students learn to internalize the steps you model and teach. It is important that kindergarteners get the opportunity to practise this with teacher facilitation. While most teachers focus on conventions (grammar, spelling, punctuation), the skill of generating ideas, organizing those ideas and selecting the key ideas is equally if not more important in learning to write succinctly.

Below you will find the graphic organizer that has been used successfully with young students. At times, pictures can be used to prompt oral rehearsal of the ideas the student has chosen to talk (or write) about. The kindergarten checklist on the next page was used to assess the samples that complete this chapter. All samples provide written comments to explain the assessment of the written work.

Kindergarten Graphic Organizer

Kindergarten Power Writing Checklist (for Teachers)

Student has demonstrated growth in the use of: *(highlight or checkmark applicable criteria)*

Ideas

- ☐ Follows modelled organizer
- ☐ Generates their own ideas for writing

Power Writing Format

- ☐ Opening sentence
- ☐ Closing sentence
- ☐ 3 supporting/related details

Word Choice

- ☐ Incorporated theme or modelled words
- ☐ Use of synonyms "Fancy Words" *(e.g. huge vs big)*
- ☐ Use of descriptive language

Attitudes

- ☐ Evidence of risk taking in their writing
- ☐ Willingness to undertake the writing task
- ☐ Understanding that their writing communicates a message
- ☐ Evidence of pride in their finish product
- ☐ Positively responds to feedback

Spelling

- ☐ Initial sounds only
- ☐ Initial and end sounds
- ☐ Phonetically recognizable words (without vowels)
- ☐ Phonetically recognizable words (with vowels)
- ☐ High frequency words spelled correctly as specified by the teacher
- ☐ Use of environmental print (e.g. classroom resources)

Conventions

- ☐ Capitals
- ☐ Spaces
- ☐ Punctuation
- ☐ Proper use of upper/lower case letters
- ☐ Left to right progression
- ☐ Correct letter orientation

Anecdotal Notes:

See *Appendix 4* for downloadable link.

Kindergarten Samples

Example 1

Transcribed: I Buttterflies dtG cpit.

Student has demonstrated growth in the use of:

Ideas	Power Writing Format	Word Choice
❑ Follows modeled organizer ❑ Generates his/her own ideas for writing	❑ Opening sentence ❑ Closing sentence ❑ 3 supporting/related details	❑ Incorporated theme or modeled words ❑ Use of synonyms "Fancy Words" (e.g. huge vs. big) ❑ Use of descriptive language

Attitudes
❑ Evidence of risk taking in his/her writing ✔ ❑ Willingness to undertake the writing task ✔ ❑ Understanding that his/her writing communicates a message ❑ Evidence of pride in his/her finished product ❑ Positively responds to feedback

Spelling	Conventions
❑ Initial sounds only ❑ Initial and end sounds ❑ Phonetically recognizable words (without vowels) ❑ Phonetically recognizable words (with vowels) ❑ High frequency words spelled correctly as specified by the teacher ✔ ❑ Use of environmental print (e.g. classroom resources) ✔	❑ Capitals ✔ ❑ Spaces ✔ ❑ Punctuation ❑ Proper use of upper and lower case letters ❑ Left to right progression WORKING ON IT ✔ ❑ Correct letter orientation

Strengths:	Next Steps:
- written attempt - copied environmental print - knows the word "I" - spaces between words - can form letters - knows groups of letters make words	- directionality (the "nd I" on the right was the first attempt) - one complete sentence - reversals - record dominant sounds in unfamiliar words

Example 2

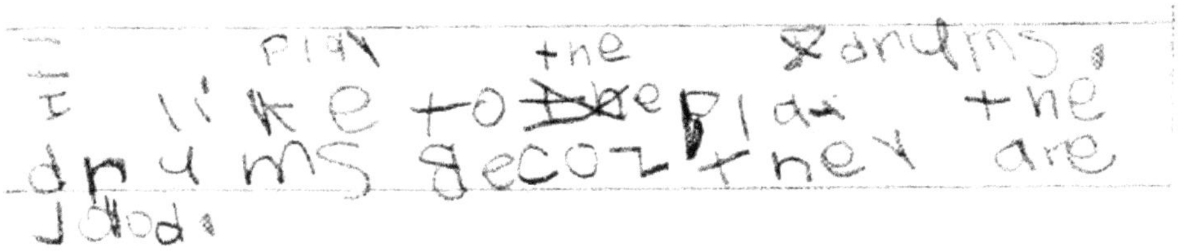

Transcribed:
I play the drums. I like to play the drumbs becoz they are laod. (loud).

Student has demonstrated growth in the use of:

Ideas	Power Writing Format	Word Choice
❑ Follows modeled organizer ❑ Generates his/her own ideas for writing ✔	❑ Opening sentence ✔ ❑ Closing sentence ❑ 3 supporting/related details ✔ (only 1 – time ran out)	❑ Incorporated theme or modeled words ❑ Use of synonyms "Fancy Words" (e.g. huge vs. big) ❑ Use of descriptive language ✔

Attitudes
❑ Evidence of risk taking in his/her writing ❑ Willingness to undertake the writing task ❑ Understanding that his/her writing communicates a message ❑ Evidence of pride in his/her finished product ❑ Positively responds to feedback ✔

Spelling	Conventions
❑ Initial sounds only ❑ Initial and end sounds ❑ Phonetically recognizable words (without vowels) ✔ ❑ Phonetically recognizable words (with vowels) ✔ ❑ High frequency words spelled correctly as specified by the teacher ✔ ❑ Use of environmental print (e.g. classroom resources) ✔	❑ Capitals ❑ Spaces WORKING ON IT ✔ ❑ Punctuation ✔ ❑ Proper use of upper and lower case letters ❑ Left to right progression ✔ ❑ Correct letter orientation

Strengths:	Next Steps:
- opening sentence - one strong detail - many conventional spellings	- letter reversal - two additional details - closing sentence - spacing

Example 3

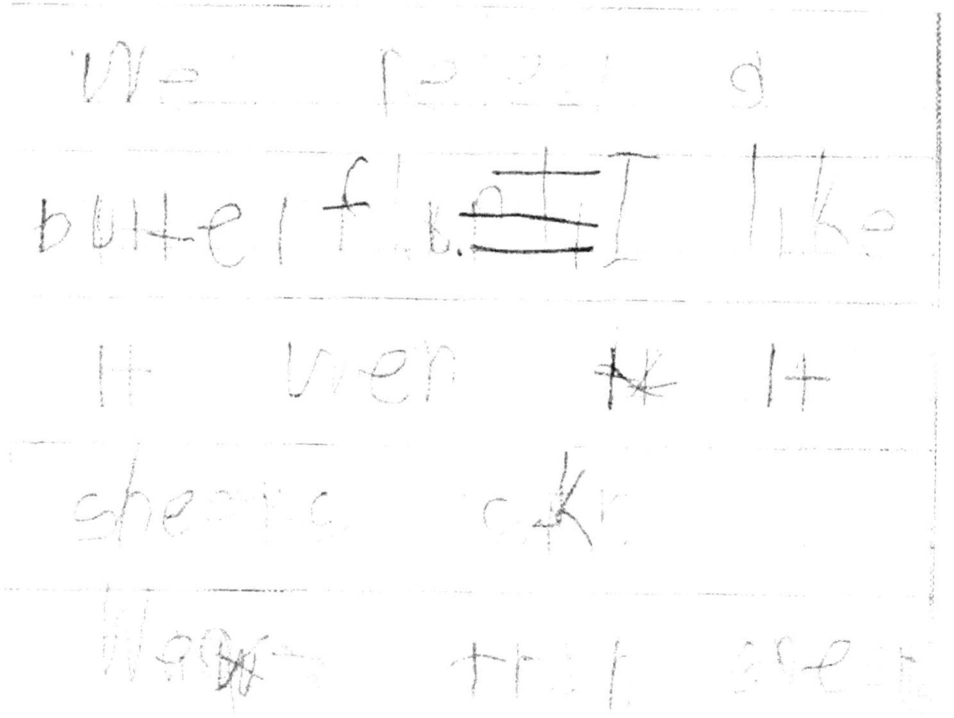

Transcribed: We relest (released) a butterfly. I like it wen it shesiss (sheds its) sikn (skin) we than snesitsy (?)

Student has demonstrated growth in the use of:

Ideas	Power Writing Format	Word Choice
❑ Follows modeled organizer (time ran out, not complete) ✓	❑ Opening sentence	❑ Incorporated theme or modeled words ✓
	❑ Closing sentence	❑ Use of synonyms "Fancy Words" (e.g. huge vs. big)
❑ Generates his/her own ideas for writing	❑ 3 supporting/related details	❑ Use of descriptive language

Attitudes
❑ Evidence of risk taking in his/her writing ✓
❑ Willingness to undertake the writing task ✓
❑ Understanding that his/her writing communicates a message ✓
❑ Evidence of pride in his/her finished product
❑ Positively responds to feedback

Spelling	Conventions
❑ Initial sounds only	❑ Capitals
❑ Initial and end sounds	❑ Spaces ✓
❑ Phonetically recognizable words (without vowels) ✓	❑ Punctuation
❑ Phonetically recognizable words (with vowels)	❑ Proper use of upper and lower case letters ✓
❑ High frequency words spelled correctly as specified by the teacher ✓	❑ Left to right progression ✓
❑ Use of environmental print (e.g. classroom resources) ✓	❑ Correct letter orientation ✓

Strengths:	Next Steps:
- word choice - vocabulary (e.g. released, sheds) is specific to subject (Science) - phonetic spelling - good spacing - opening sentence - one detail sentence	- capitalization - additional sentences to follow (organizer 1, 2, 2, 1)

Example 4

Transcribed: I like lizzards. Lizzards look spiky. Some eat draginflys. lizards are amazing.

Student has demonstrated growth in the use of:

Ideas	Power Writing Format	Word Choice
❑ Follows modeled organizer ✓ ❑ Generates his/her own ideas for writing	❑ Opening sentence ✓ ❑ Closing sentence ✓ ❑ 3 supporting/related details	❑ Incorporated theme or modeled words ✓ ❑ Use of synonyms "Fancy Words" (e.g. huge vs. big) ✓ ❑ Use of descriptive language

Attitudes
❑ Evidence of risk taking in his/her writing ❑ Willingness to undertake the writing task ❑ Understanding that his/her writing communicates a message ❑ Evidence of pride in his/her finished product ❑ Positively responds to feedback ✓

Spelling	Conventions
❑ Initial sounds only ❑ Initial and end sounds ❑ Phonetically recognizable words (without vowels) ✓ ❑ Phonetically recognizable words (with vowels) ❑ High frequency words spelled correctly as specified by the teacher ✓ ❑ Use of environmental print (e.g. classroom resources) ✓	❑ Capitals ❑ Spaces ❑ Punctuation ❑ Proper use of upper and lower case letters ❑ Left to right progression ❑ Correct letter orientation ✓

Strengths:	Next Steps:
- sentence variety (simple) - word choice (e.g. spikey) - two distinct details - opening/closing sentences	- add another power 2 so it would be 1, 2, 2, 2, 1 - conventions – capitalization in appropriate places

Example 5

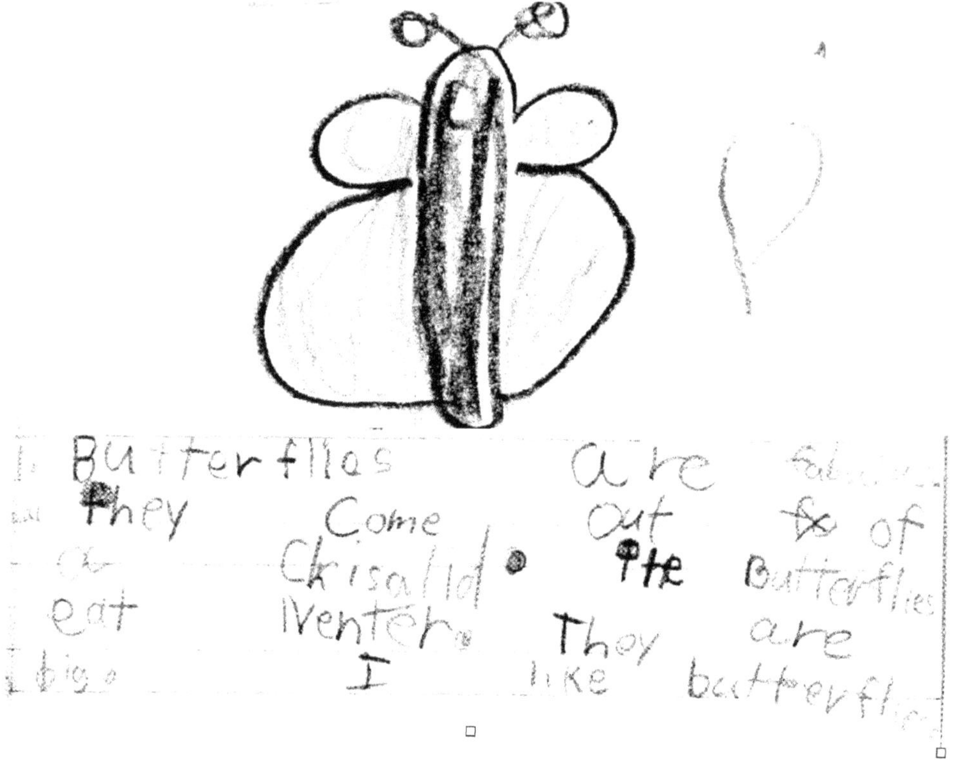

Transcribed: Butterflies are fabuluse They come out of a Chrisalid. The Butterflies eat iventer. They are big. I like butterflies.

Student has demonstrated growth in the use of:

Ideas	Power Writing Format	Word Choice
❑Follows modeled organizer ✓ ❑Generates his/her own ideas for writing	❑Opening sentence ❑Closing sentence ❑3 supporting/related details	❑Incorporated theme or modeled words ✓ ❑Use of synonyms "Fancy Words" (e.g. huge vs. big) ✓ ❑Use of descriptive language

Attitudes
❑Evidence of risk taking in his/her writing ❑Willingness to undertake the writing task ❑Understanding that his/her writing communicates a message ❑Evidence of pride in his/her finished product ❑Positively responds to feedback ✓

Spelling	Conventions
❑Initial sounds only ❑Initial and end sounds ❑Phonetically recognizable words (without vowels) ✓ ❑Phonetically recognizable words (with vowels) ✓ ❑High frequency words spelled correctly as specified by the teacher ✓ ❑Use of environmental print (e.g. classroom resources) ✓	❑Capitals ❑Spaces ❑Punctuation ❑Proper use of upper and lower case letters ❑Left to right progression ❑Correct letter orientation ✓

Strengths:	Next Steps:
- periods - word choice (e.g. fabulous) - space - conventions (capitals) - 3 distinct ideas - opening/closing sentence - three Power 2s	- refine capitalization practices - additional practise applying what student already knows - continued work on word choice (e.g. big -> huge; like -> admire)

Example 6

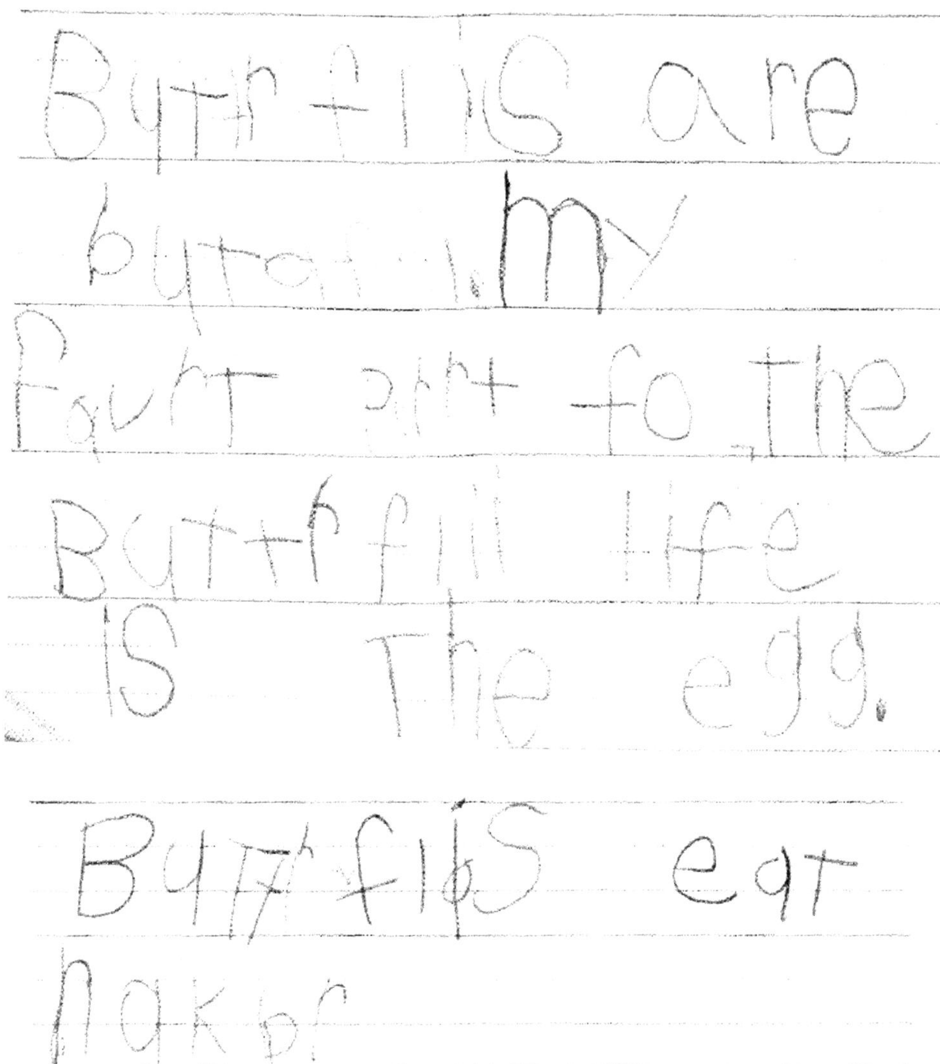

Transcribed: Buttrflis are butafel (Butterflies are beautiful). My favrt part fo the Buttrflii life is the egg. (My favourite part of the butterfly's life is the egg). Buttifliis eat nakar (Butterflies eat nectar).

Student has demonstrated growth in the use of:

Ideas	Power Writing Format	Word Choice
❑ Follows modeled organizer ❑ Generates his/her own ideas for writing	❑ Opening sentence ❑ Closing sentence ❑ 3 supporting/related details (2 details, ran out of time)	❑ Incorporated theme or modeled words ❑ Use of synonyms "Fancy Words" (e.g. huge vs. big) ❑ Use of descriptive language

Attitudes
❑ Evidence of risk taking in his/her writing ❑ Willingness to undertake the writing task ❑ Understanding that his/her writing communicates a message ❑ Evidence of pride in his/her finished product ❑ Positively responds to feedback

Spelling	Conventions
❑ Initial sounds only ❑ Initial and end sounds ❑ Phonetically recognizable words (without vowels) ❑ Phonetically recognizable words (with vowels) ❑ High frequency words spelled correctly as specified by the teacher ❑ Use of environmental print (e.g. classroom resources)	❑ Capitals ❑ Spaces ❑ Punctuation ❑ Proper use of upper and lower case letters ❑ Left to right progression ❑ Correct letter orientation

Strengths:	Next Steps:
- incorporated subject specific vocabulary (e.g. "life" nectar) - follows modeled	- closing sentence - refine capitalization

Summary

The above samples provide a glimpse into what kindergarteners are capable of once you model and teach the Power Writing process. The variety of results is the spectrum of students you may have as well as the school-year progression you may observe. Use the samples to inform your practice and guide your instruction.

CHAPTER FOUR

Elementary

Literacy skills, especially reading, aid students in understanding the written structure. Students in the early years of elementary schooling are focused on learning to read. In the later years, students read to learn. They need to understand the written structure to develop their own writing skills. The cycle of direct instruction, practise, and feedback is ideal for students to become writers. As you are well aware, not everything needs to be marked. Elementary students are not yet in the abstract thinking stage. They are very much concrete learners. Students shouldn't be guessing what the teacher is asking for when they have to complete a task. So be clear, model expectations and allow for lots of practise.

Having clear criteria for students help them self-monitor. Rubrics are not only helpful for self-evaluation as the student progresses through an assignment, it makes for easy assessment and evaluation when an assignment is submitted. You are already familiar with the graphic organizers that elementary students can use for the 1-2-2-2-1 and 1-2-3-2-3-2-3-1 patterns. For ease, they are included below. The following pages detail the rubric used to evaluate the samples in this chapter. You would simplify it to be age-appropriate for your students. Re-read the section on rubrics in the *Introduction* if you require a refresher of its structure. Remember you can alter the rubric to meet your specific assignment needs (see Appendix 4).

Power Writing Graphic Organizer

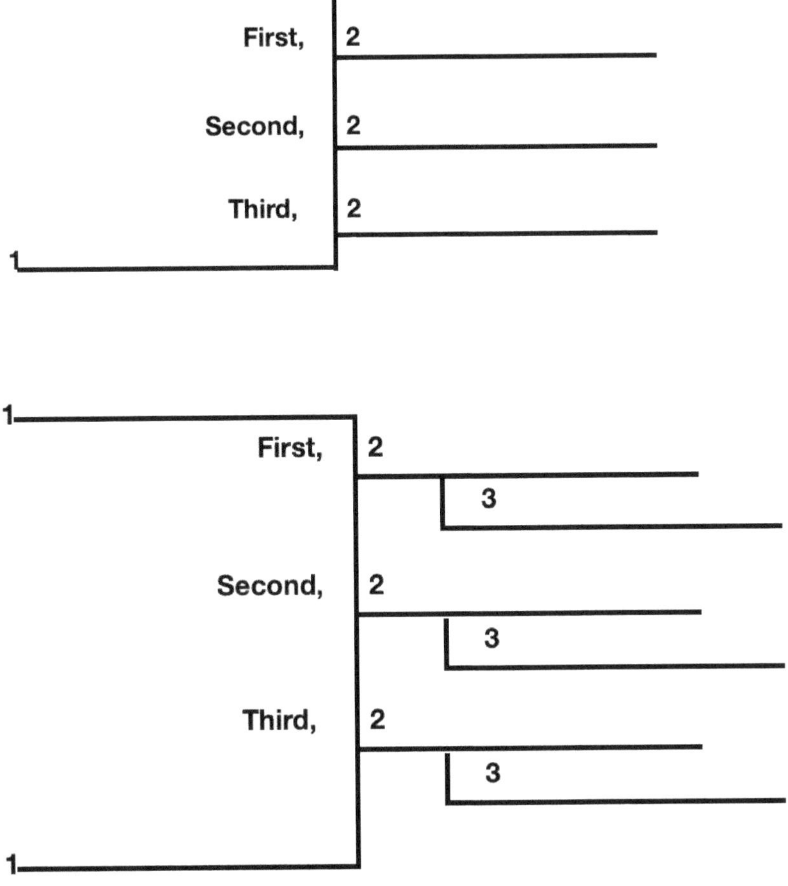

Categories	Expectations	Level 4	Level 3	Level 2	Level 1
Graphic Organizer	Organizer is followed to generate introduction and supporting ideas	Details connect **specifically** to the main idea. Details are purposefully linked. The graphic organizer is thoughtful and focused.	Details connect **directly** to the main idea. There is a clear link between the details.	Details connect to the main idea. The relationship between the ideas are unclear or the ideas don't match.	Includes main idea. Details lack connection to the main idea.
IDEAS	Power 1 and 2 *Here you would include examples of the topic*	Pets Kitten Puppy Hamster Pets	Animals Kitten Puppy Cub Animals	Animals Kitten Bear Furry Animals	Animals Love them Eat Zoo Animals
	Power 1, 2 and 3 (after mastering Power 1 and 2) *Here you would include examples of the topic*	Pets Kitten Claws at fishbowl Puppy Chews socks Hamster Burrows a nest Pets	Pets Kitten Purs & meows Puppy Licks face Cub Runs in wheel Pets	Pets Kitten Muffin Bear Small Furry Eats pellets Pets	Pets Kitten Puppy Brown Hamster No Pets
Power 1 ORGANIZATION	Main Idea - topic sentence refers to first and last sentence	Topic sentences are **exceptionally clear** and connected to the main idea.	Topic sentences are **well stated**. The last sentence is linked to the main idea (or vice-versa)	Topic sentence is **clear**. The last sentence does not relate back to the main idea (or vice-versa).	Topic and/or last sentence is **unclear.** There is no topic/last sentence. Not sure what the main idea is.
Power 2	Major Details	Paragraph has **three** detail sentences which **strongly** connect to the main idea.	Paragraph has **three** supporting detail sentences which **relate well** to the main idea.	Paragraph has minimum **two** supporting detail sentences which relate somewhat back to the main idea.	Paragraph has **one** supporting detail sentence which attempts to relate back to the main idea.
Power 3	Minor Details connecting to Power 2	Paragraph has **three or more** detail sentences which **strongly and clearly** connect to *Power 2*. The sentences flow like you're talking.	Paragraph has **three** detail sentences that each extend upon *Power 2*. The sentences flow one to another and ideas are mostly connected.	Paragraph has minimum **two** detail sentences that extend upon a *Power 2*. The ideas between Power 2s and Power 3s are not always connected.	Paragraph has **one or more** detail sentences but the ideas do not connect to the *Power 2*.

Categories	Expectations	Level 4	Level 3	Level 2	Level 1
Power 0 **V** **O**	Catchy phrase or hook linked to the topic sentence.	The hook "wows" the reader (i.e. makes them laugh, respond, question etc.). Connects perfectly with the paragraph.	The hook grabs the reader's attention and fits well with the paragraph.	The hook fits but needs to be more specific to the topic.	The hook seems out of place and is not effective. It does not grab the reader's attention for the right reasons.
Voice **I** **C** **E**	My personal mark is left.	Uses two or more of the following: Questions, sound words, human characteristics to non-human things or similes.	The paragraph asks questions, or uses sound words, or gives human characteristics to non-human things or uses "like" or "as" to compare two things.	Attempts to use questions or sound words (e.g. snap, buzz, pop) to bring their personal feeling into their writing.	No attempt to use questions or sound words.
Fluency	The smoothness and flow of the written piece.	It is easy to read the sentences aloud. Sentence beginnings are interesting and varied. The sentences are different lengths.	Sentences are well built. It is easy to read the sentences aloud. Sentence beginnings are interesting. The sentences are different lengths.	There are some places to make smoother when I read aloud. Attempts to begin sentences in different ways. Blend or separate some sentences to make the different lengths	The sentences aren't working well. It is difficult to read the paragraph aloud as it needs to be smoother. The beginnings all sound the same. Too much use of "*and*".
Word Choice	Effective word choice.	Word choice includes **exceptional** transition words, a variety of descriptive and action words. A vivid picture is created for the reader.	Word choice includes various transition, descriptive and action words. Creates a clear picture for the reader.	Word choice is **adequate** because it adds only a bit of details. Uses familiar transition words. The reader begins to create a picture in their mind.	Word choice is **simple** and **repetitive**. Uses modelled transition words (e.g. Firstly, Secondly, Thirdly). The reader has a difficult time painting a picture in their mind.
Conventions	Mechanics are correct.	Paragraph has no punctuation, capitalization, grammar and spelling errors.	Paragraph has **very few** punctuation, capitalization, grammar and spelling errors.	Paragraph has **several** punctuation, capitalization, grammar and spelling errors.	Paragraph has **many** punctuation, capitalization, grammar and spelling errors.

See *Appendix 4* for downloadable link.

2 of 2

Elementary Samples

Example 1

Evaluated Level 2-

Power Writing　　　　Name Mason

1. lat th the zoo

Firstly. 2. Play

Secondly. 2. ribaing riding animals

Thirdly. 2. sers exploring

1.

lat. ih the zoo

If my friends and I were locked in all night these thee things would be so much fun to do.

Firstly play in the zoo won bee fun we woo play tag

Secondly riding anmils won be cool and fun.

Thirdly aspirine wab be sowt wen woo fint fas

the zoo is cool.

Transcribed:

Locked in the Zoo

If my friends and I were locked in all night these three things would the so much to do.

Firstly play in the zoo would be fun we would play tag.
Secondly riding animals would be cool and fun.

Thirdly exploring would be sowt (?) we would find fas(?).
The zoo is cool.

Next Steps:

This student has used the graphic organizer to organize the paragraph. From the sample, the student requires guidance and practice in constructing sentences (i.e. varying length and various structure). Although the ideas are present in the written work, it is difficult to read and comprehend and thus the teacher would support this student with providing word processing tools (e.g. spell prediction programs, word wall/list) to practise sight words and word-families.

Example 2

Evaluated Level 2

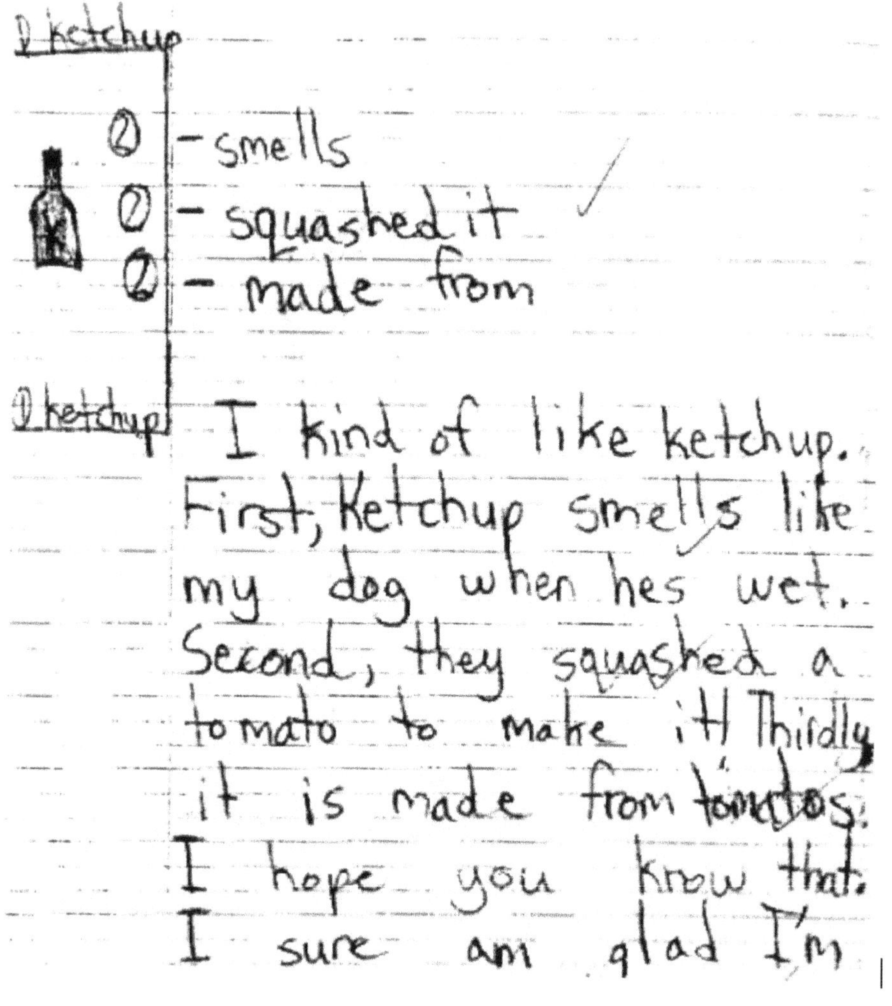

not a tomato.

Transcribed:

I kind of like ketchup.
First, Ketchup smells like my dog when he's wet.
Second, they squashed a tomato to make it!. Thirdly,
it is made from tomatos.
I hope you know that.
I sure am glad I'm not a tomato.

Next Steps:

The graphic organizer, although correctly completed, lacks interconnection between the ideas at the Power 2 level. The teacher would therefore support this student by modelling and practising categorizing and linking ideas. The goal is to help the student focus on three main points but this will require the organizer to have three linked ideas. Although the sentence "I hope you know that." appears to add *voice* it is not needed and does not tightly fit into the paragraph (i.e. it serves no purpose). Finally, the closing sentence does not directly tie back to the main idea.

Example 3

Evaluated Level 2+

diesel
2 cute
2 biting
2 fast
diesel

We grot our puppy From a house. First, my puppy is so cute that I feel like squeezing him. Second, every time I put on my coat he starts biting me hard Third, when I go in the backyard I start to run then he starts to run after me and trys to bite me. Diesel was born 2 weeks ago in a house.

Transcribed:

We got our puppy From a house. First. my puppy is so cute that I feel like squeezing him. Second, every time I put on my coat he starts biting me hard. Third, when I go in the backyard I start to run then he starts to run after me and try to bite me. Diesel was born 2 weeks ago in a house.

Next Steps:

Although this student has included the graphic organizer, it needs to be clearer and the ideas should be used in the paragraph. Again, as in the previous example, the teacher would assist this student by helping the student categorize and link the Power 2 ideas through modelling and lots of cross-curricular practise. In this example, the opening sentence needs to be clearly stated as the reader is not sure what this paragraph will be about (i.e. Diesel is not mentioned). The teacher would assist the student in writing clearer topic sentences that introduce the main idea to the reader. Likewise, the closing sentence does not summarize what is in the paragraph and lacks connection to the topic sentence. Modelling correct conventions and providing avenues to discover new and better, more accurate word-choices for the grade level will also benefit this student's learning.

Example 4

Evaluated Level 3-

Power Writing Name: Charlotte

Locked in school

2. Staf room

Firstly,

2. do work in class ro

Secondly

2. drink all milk I want to drink

Thirdly

1. lock in school

Locked In School

If my friends and I were LOCKED in school all night long, these three things would be so much fun to do. To begin with, it would be hilarious to go into the staff room because it would be witty to preatend we're a teacher. Next, it would be so much rip-roarin to work in the class room all night long

Most importantly, I can go in
The kichen, and drink all the
milk we wont to drink, and
me and my friends can cook
and be a chef for the night.
No closing sentence
That's what I would do if
I was locked in on this
fantastick night! THE END

Transcribed:

If my friends and I were LOCKED in school all night long these three things would be SO much fun to do. To begin with, it would be hilarious to go into the staff room because, it would be witty to preatend we're a teacher. Next, it would be so much rip-roarin to work in the class from all night long. Most importantly, I can go in the kitchen, and drink all the milk we want to drink, and me and my friends can cook and be a chef for the night. That's what I would do if I was locked in on this fantastic night! THE END

Next Steps:

The student has demonstrated the ability to organize thoughts in a graphic organizer. The teacher may want to model and demonstrate how to choose specific Power 2 words in the organizer so the student stays focused on those ideas. Take note of the second sentence that reads "To begin with, it would be...because, it would be witty to preatend we're a teacher." Power Writing suggests not using the word *because* as it naturally lends to providing more details which then becomes a Power 3. The word *because* in this instance takes away from details that the Power 3 would provide (and may create a habit of run-on sentences similarly to the word *and* or *then*). Furthermore, this student could use assistance with word-choice in that the uses of *witty* and *rip-roarin* do not fit the context of the sentence. Finally, this student would also benefit from explicit teaching in formulating closing sentences.

Example 5

Evaluated Level 3

1. Valentines day
cops
candy
cards
Valentines dance
1. Valentines day

Valentines day rocks! Would you like to hear about valentines day? First, sometimes the candy is carmel my favorite filling in candy. Second, you get to get cards that sometimes has a picture of a dog or a cat. Third I Love the valentines dance because I have lots

of friends to dance with

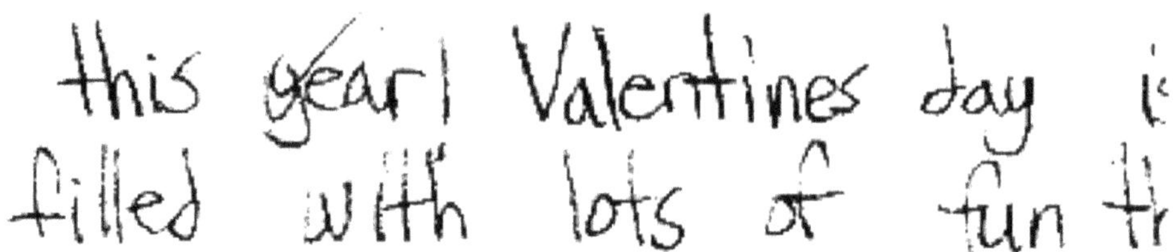

Transcribed:

Valentine's day rocks! Would you like to hear about valentines day? First, sometimes the candy is carmel my favourite filling in candy. Second, you get to get cards that some-times has a picture of a dog or a cat. Third, I Love the valentines (dance) because I have lots of friends to dance with this year! Valentines day is filled with lots of fun things.

Next Steps:

This student has written a paragraph from the ideas generated in the graphic organizer. Although the graphic organizer is missing transition words, the paragraph includes them. It meets Level 3 criteria. A teacher may want to model various lengths of sentences and Power 3 details to have this student progress in his/her ability to write.

Example 6

Evaluated Level 3+

on [illegible] [illegible]ible
on

Its brown Its round
and it makes me cry! Todays
worst vegetible is...... Onions!
First, when I'm haveing dinner
onions somehow sneak out of
the pan onto my plate and
onto my fork. Second, Onions
make me ball my eyes out!
Third, They are so horible
I will never ever look onions
again! When your parents
make you eat onions, protest
convice them that frys are better

Transcribed:

It's brown. It's round and it makes me cry! Todays worst vegetable is..... Onions! First, when I'm haveing dinner onions somehow sneak out of the pan onto my plate and onto my fork. Second, Onions make me ball my eyes out! Third, They are so horrible I will never ever look onions again! When your parents make you eat onions, please convince them that frys are better.

Next Steps:

This student has demonstrated original voice, used Power Zero to capture the reader's attention, and used similes to create a picture in the reader's mind. A teacher may guide this student to be more accurate when self-editing (especially conventions) and provide a challenging topic that may not be a personal experience and may require persuasive writing.

Example 7
Evaluated Level 4

Teacher — Homework — Name — Jellybean — Teacher

Yum!

My teacher Mrs. LeClair is the best and I say the best teacher in Gr.3 First, she helps me with my homework alot of the time and keep this a secret from my mom sometimes she

gives me the answers. Second,
her name is Mrs. Le Clair;
her real name is Mary
Zanellato. Third, she gives me
jellybeans when I am very, very
good but I have not gotten
a jellybean in a long time;
that means I have not been
good enough. My teacher
Mrs. Le Clair is the **best**
Gr. 3 teacher in the world.

Transcribed:

Yum! My teacher Mrs. LeClair is the best and I say the best teacher in Gr. 3. First, she helps me with my homework alot of the time and keep this a secret from my mom sometimes she gives me the answers. Second, her name is Mrs. LeClair her real name is Mary Zanellato. Third, she gives me jellybeans when I am very, very good but I have not gotten a jelly bean in a long time; that means I have not been good enough. My teacher Mrs. LeClair is the best Gr. 3 teacher in the world.

Next Steps:

You really notice the student's ability to use voice in this paragraph. For example, the first Power 2 illustrates the student's awareness of audience, "…keep this a secret from my mom…". To further develop this student's ability, modelling a variation of word-choice and providing a topic challenge in various genres will benefit his/her learning.

Example 8

Evaluated Level 4

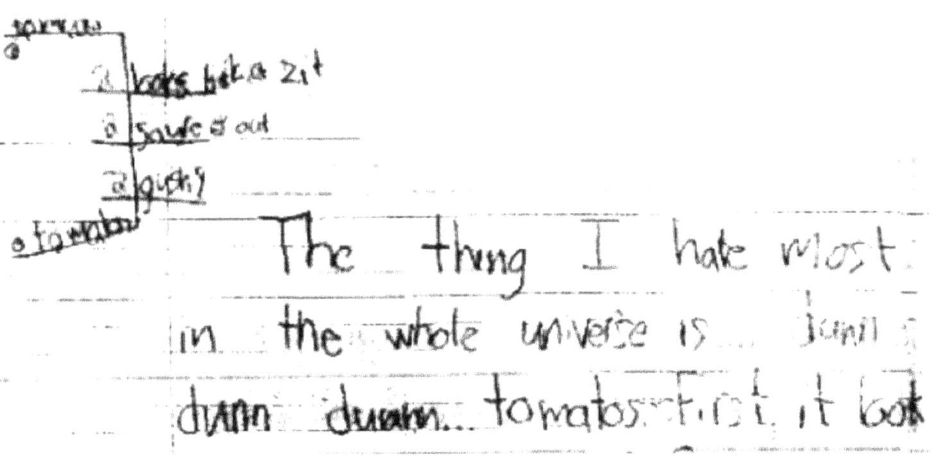

The thing I hate most in the whole universe is … tomatos. First, it look

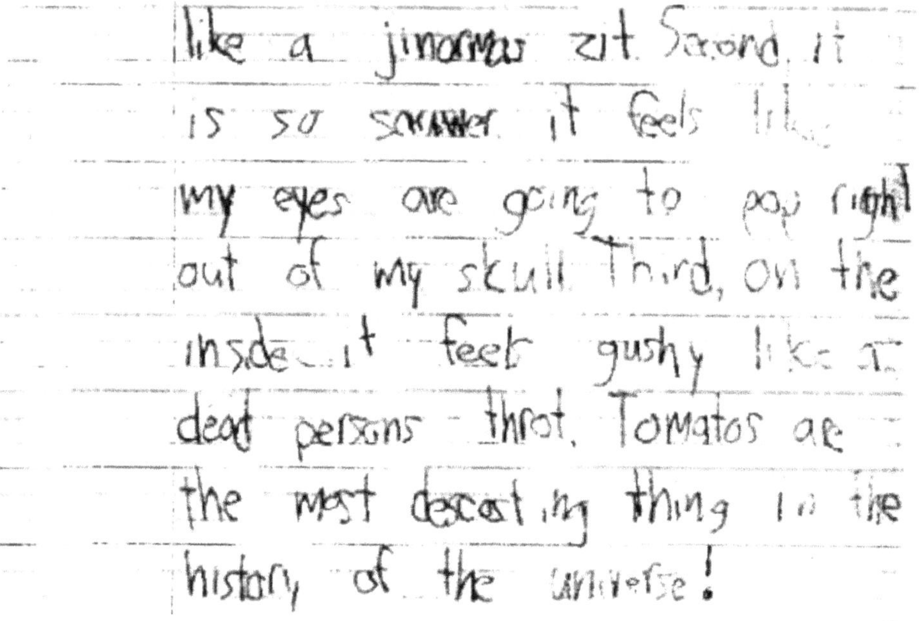

Transcribed:

The thing I hate most in the whole universe is…. dunn dunn dum… tomatos. First, it look like a jinormas zit. Second it is so sauwer it feels like my eyes are going to pop right out of my skull. Third, on the inside it feels gushy like a dead person's throt. Tomatos are the most descosting thing in the history of the universe!

Next Steps:

As mentioned in the previous examples, this student has demonstrated original voice, used Power Zero to capture the reader's attention, and created a picture in the reader's mind. A teacher may guide this student by providing a challenging topic that may require further research beyond the personal experience or opinion (e.g. narrative, persuasive argument, letter etc.). Although there are spelling errors (tomatoes, enormous, sour, throat, disgusting) which would have resulted a level 2 evaluation, the other rubric categories demonstrated a consistent level 4. This would therefore bring the written piece to an overall score of level 4 as the most consistent performance.

Summary

The elementary samples provide you with what students may produce after you have taught them the power writing process. It is important to note that a simplified rubric or criteria checklist be provided for the students so they can self-assess and peer-assess each other's work. It is also important to provide such concrete, clear expectations so that the elementary student, who has not yet reached the developmental stage of abstract thinking, knows exactly what they are working toward.

The rubric provided is a starting point for you and can be modified to fit your needs. You would adjust the samples in the "ideas" section, specifically Power 2 and Power 3, depending on the topic and your guided writing facilitation when modelling power writing. Feel free to use the same topics as in the samples and show the samples to your students. Perhaps you would evaluate the samples differently than what is labelled here, using the same rubric. That is fine. The point is that you can validate your assessment with the criteria listed in your rubric. That is the professional judgement afforded to you as a teacher.

CHAPTER FIVE

Middle-School

Even if middle-schoolers have never been exposed to power writing in previous grades, the process will break unproductive habits and get the most reluctant writer to produce a concise paragraph. What is even more advantageous is that middle-schoolers can use this process in all subjects to communicate their knowledge and application of new concepts learned. Students in the middle-school grades are reading to learn and are exposed to more abstract concepts. They are being asked to think and connect these concepts to their own lives and beyond.

You are familiar with the graphic organizers that show pattern 1-2-2-2-1, 1-2-3-2-3-2-3-1 and equally with power zero at the beginning 0-1-2-3-2-3-2-3-1. The rubric used to evaluate the samples in this chapter look for the most consistent level of performance in all categories. Hence, if a student performs for example a level 2 for conventions but in all other categories performs at a level 4, the most consistent level becomes the overall score. In this example that would be level 4. If you need a refresher on what the levels equate to in letter grades or percentages, re-read the *Introduction* for a detailed description. Remember you can modify the rubric provided in the next few pages to fit your own needs and provide a simplified version for your students to use for self-assessment.

Power Writing Graphic Organizer

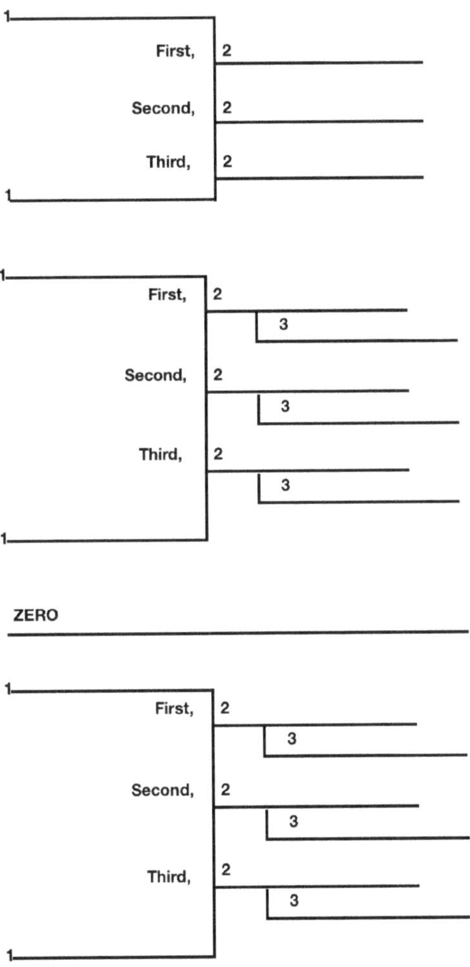

Categories	Expectations	Level 4	Level 3	Level 2	Level 1
Graphic Organizer	Organizer is followed to generate introduction and supporting ideas	Details connect **specifically** to the main idea. Details are purposefully linked. The graphic organizer is thoughtful and focused.	Details connect **directly** to the main idea. There is a clear link between the details.	Details connect to the main idea. The relationship between the ideas are unclear or the ideas don't match.	Includes main idea. Details lack connection to the main idea.
IDEAS	Power 1 and 2 *Here you would include examples of the topic*	Pets Kitten Puppy Hamster Pets	Animals Kitten Puppy Cub Animals	Animals Kitten Bear Furry Animals	Animals Love them Eat Zoo Animals
	Power 1, 2 and 3 (after mastering Power 1 and 2) *Here you would include examples of the topic*	Pets Kitten Claws at fishbowl Puppy Chews socks Hamster Burrows a nest Pets	Pets Kitten Purs & meows Puppy Licks face Cub Runs in wheel Pets	Pets Kitten Muffin Bear Small Furry Eats pellets Pets	Pets Kitten Puppy Brown Hamster No Pets
Power 1 (ORGANIZATION)	Main Idea - topic sentence refers to first and last sentence	Topic sentences are **exceptionally clear** and connected to the main idea.	Topic sentences are **well stated**. The last sentence is linked to the main idea (or vice-versa)	Topic sentence is **clear**. The last sentence does not relate back to the main idea (or vice-versa).	Topic and/or last sentence is **unclear.** There is no topic/last sentence. Not sure what the main idea is.
Power 2	Major Details	Paragraph has **three** detail sentences which **strongly** connect to the main idea.	Paragraph has **three** supporting detail sentences which **relate well** to the main idea.	Paragraph has minimum **two** supporting detail sentences which relate somewhat back to the main idea.	Paragraph has **one** supporting detail sentence which attempts to relate back to the main idea.
Power 3	Minor Details connecting to Power 2	Paragraph has **three or more** detail sentences which **strongly and clearly** connect to *Power 2*. The sentences flow like you're talking.	Paragraph has **three** detail sentences that each extend upon *Power 2*. The sentences flow one to another and ideas are mostly connected.	Paragraph has minimum **two** detail sentences that extend upon a *Power 2*. The ideas between Power 2s and Power 3s are not always connected.	Paragraph has **one or more** detail sentences but the ideas do not connect to the *Power 2*.

Categories	Expectations	Level 4	Level 3	Level 2	Level 1
Power 0 V O	Catchy phrase or hook linked to the topic sentence.	The hook “wows” the reader (i.e. makes them laugh, respond, question etc.). Connects perfectly with the paragraph.	The hook grabs the reader’s attention and fits well with the paragraph.	The hook fits but needs to be more specific to the topic.	The hook seems out of place and is not effective. It does not grab the reader’s attention for the right reasons.
Voice I C E	My personal mark is left.	Uses two or more of the following: Questions, sound words, human characteristics to non-human things or similes.	The paragraph asks questions, or uses sound words, or gives human characteristics to non-human things or uses “like” or “as” to compare two things.	Attempts to use questions or sound words (e.g. snap, buzz, pop) to bring their personal feeling into their writing.	No attempt to use questions or sound words.
Fluency	The smoothness and flow of the written piece.	It is easy to read the sentences aloud. Sentence beginnings are interesting and varied. The sentences are different lengths.	Sentences are well built. It is easy to read the sentences aloud. Sentence beginnings are interesting. The sentences are different lengths.	There are some places to make smoother when I read aloud. Attempts to begin sentences in different ways. Blend or separate some sentences to make the different lengths	The sentences aren’t working well. It is difficult to read the paragraph aloud as it needs to be smoother. The beginnings all sound the same. Too much use of “*and*”.
Word Choice	Effective word choice.	Word choice includes **exceptional** transition words, a variety of descriptive and action words. A vivid picture is created for the reader.	Word choice includes various transition, descriptive and action words. Creates a clear picture for the reader.	Word choice is **adequate** because it adds only a bit of details. Uses familiar transition words. The reader begins to create a picture in their mind.	Word choice is **simple** and **repetitive**. Uses modelled transition words (e.g. Firstly, Secondly, Thirdly). The reader has a difficult time painting a picture in their mind.
Conventions	Mechanics are correct.	Paragraph has no punctuation, capitalization, grammar and spelling errors.	Paragraph has **very few** punctuation, capitalization, grammar and spelling errors.	Paragraph has **several** punctuation, capitalization, grammar and spelling errors.	Paragraph has **many** punctuation, capitalization, grammar and spelling errors.

Middle-School Samples

Example 1

Evaluated Level 2-

Power Writing - A Character

1. Lizzie
- To begin with — 2. Lizzie at Last
  - 3. Exciting
- Also — 2. First day
  - 3. She bought clothes
- Finally — 2. Cladia milk
  - 3. more books

1. Lizzie

this book is so awesome I want to scream. Lizzie is the main charitor and she has not done alot of stuff in her life. To begin with my book is cald Lizzie at last. Im only half way the book and its so exciting. Also the first day of school she dosen no what to where. So she bys clothes that she does not like to where. Fianally the athor name is Cladia Mill and she sound really fun writer. So I want to find more book the She writes so I can read them. Lizzie is my favorite charitor in my book!

Transcribed:

This book is so awesome I want to scream. Lizzie is the main chariter and she has not done alot of stuff in her life. To begin with my book is cald Lizzie at last. Im only half way the book and its so exciting. Also the first day of school she dose no what to where. So she bys clothes that she does not like to where. Fianally the athor name is Cladia mill and she sound really fun writer. So I want to find more book the she writes so I can read them. Lizzie is my favourite charitor in my book!

Next Steps:

The student created a graphic organizer and the paragraph reflects that the student followed the 1, 2, 3, 2, 3, 2, 3, 1 pattern. Also, each idea was checked off as she wrote a sentence that corresponded to the ideas in the graphic organizer. Transition words were included for the Power 2 sentences. However, the details (Power 2s and 3s) do not link to the main idea (i.e. the main character Lizzi). A reader would expect the paragraph to focus on Lizzi's characteristics or actions. The student brainstormed ideas that do not link to the main idea nor interlink between one another. Explicit teaching would occur at the brainstorming and creation of the graphic organizer before having this student produce a written paragraph. It is evident that the student will easily follow the Power Writing pattern once she can independently generate ideas that are purposefully linked and are directly related to the main idea. Conventions such as spelling need to be addressed as well.

Example 2

Evaluation Level 2

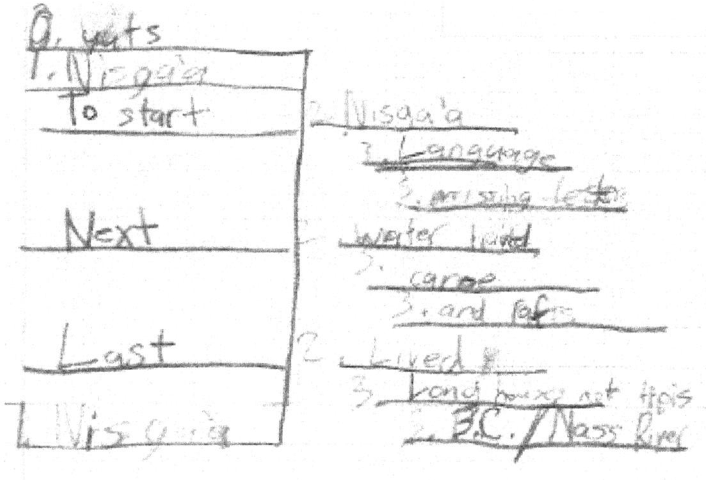

Wow!, I never Knew "uts" means bird in the Nisga'a's language. To start, Nisga'a is a native indian trib ~~that~~ spoke a different language than French or English even know their a canadian trib. A really cool thing about the Nisga'a language, is that their alphebet is missing the letters f, r, v and z. Next, did you know that the Nisga'a traveled in water by caneo and by rafts. Last, the Nisga'a lived in Long houses made of wood and did not live in tipi's. The Nisga'a lived in British-Columbia on the Nass River. Those are thing I learned about the Nisga'a indians.

Transcribed:

Wow! I never knew 'nuts" means bird in the Nisga'a's language. To start, Nisga'a is a native indian trib that spoke a different language than French or English even know their a Canadian trib. A really cool thing about the Nisga'a language, is that their alphabet is missing the letters f, r, v and z. Next, did you know that the Nisga'a travled in water by caneo and by rafts. Last, the Nisga'a lived in Long houses made of wood and did not live in tipi's. The Nisga'a lived in British-Columbia on the Nass River. Those are thing I learned about the Nisga'a indians.

Next Steps:

This student has included a Power Zero and loosely followed the ideas from the graphic organizer. This student has also used simple transition words to mark the next Power 2. Next steps includeds explicit teaching of the Power 2 and Power 3 pattern. From the example, the second Power 2 is not clearly evident and the two Power 3s have been combined into one sentence. The teacher should guide the student to writing independent sentences for each Power 3. The student also needs guidance to improve his/her application of conventions.

Example 3

Evaluated Level 2

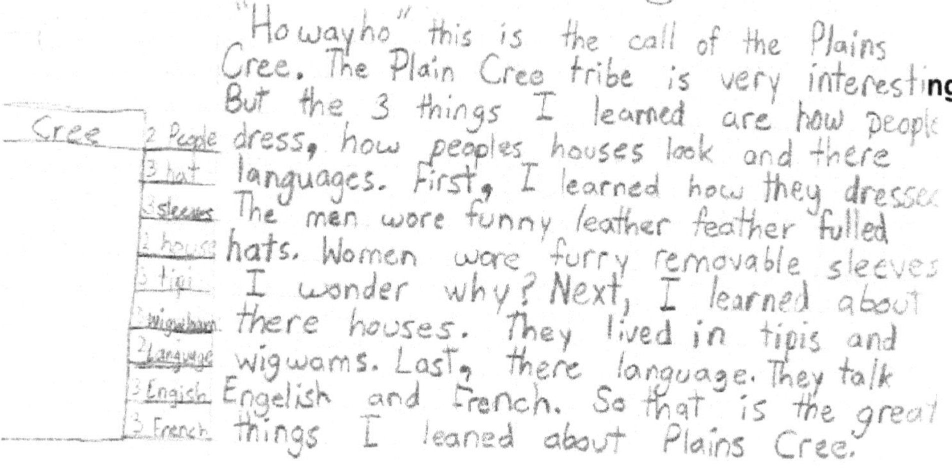

Transcribed:

"Ho wayho" this is the call of the Plains Cree. The Plain Cree tribe is very interesting. But the 3 things I learned are how people dress, how peoples houses look and there languages. First, I learned how they dressed. The men wore funny leather feather fulled hats. Women wore furry removable sleeves. I wonder why? Next, I learned about there houses. They lived in tipis and wigwams. Last, there language. They talk Engelish and French. So that is the great things I leaned about Plans Cree.

Next Steps:

The example includes a Power 0 that captures the reader's attention. The student has included the basic transition words and all ideas from the graphic organizer are included in the paragraph. Next steps for this student include explicit teaching of a more concise

Power 1 sentence. In this example, it is unclear whether the Power 1 begins with the sentence "But..." or includes the preceding sentence (i.e. "The Plain Cree..."). The second and third Power 2 combines Power 3s in one sentence. These ideas should be written as separate sentences. The student requires explicit teaching of sentence structure (e.g. "Last, there language." [sic]) and conventions (e.g. grammar – the student writes "there" for their and "talk" for speak).

Example 4

Evaluated Level 3

1. Good best friend

First | 2. nice | 3. talk & play

I also | 2. honest | 3. no gossip

Above all | 2. respectful | 3. me & others (+) things

1. Good best friend

"Thats okay, I understand". Best friends are hard to find but when you do they should have these qualities. First, I look for someone who is nice. I want to talk and play with them everyday (especially at school). I also think a friend needs to be honest. For example they wouldnt gossip about you behind your back. Above all, they need to be respectful. Not just to you but to your belongings and others around you. If your friend has all three of these qualities you know you have a really good, true friend!

Transcribed:

"That's okay. I understand." Best friends are hard to find but when you do they should have these qualities. First, I look for someone who is nice. I want to talk and play with them everyday (especially at school). I also think a friend needs to be honest. For example they wouldn't gossip about you behind your back. Above all, they need to be respectful. Not just to you but your belongings and others around you. If your friend has all three of these qualities you know you have a really good, true friend!

Next Steps:

This example demonstrates that the student has created a graphic organizer that demonstrates Power 2s and 3s linking directly to the main idea. The student has chosen common transition words. The effective use of a Power 0 adds to the overall impact of the paragraph. Both Power 1 sentences are well stated and clearly reflect the main idea. Only minor errors in conventions are noted. Next steps for this student is to choose more specific transition words and more sophisticated word choices (e.g. a better descriptor for "nice"). Although this example shows various sentence starters, student should be cautioned to avoid sentence fragments (e.g. "Not just to you…").

Example 5

Evaluated Level 3

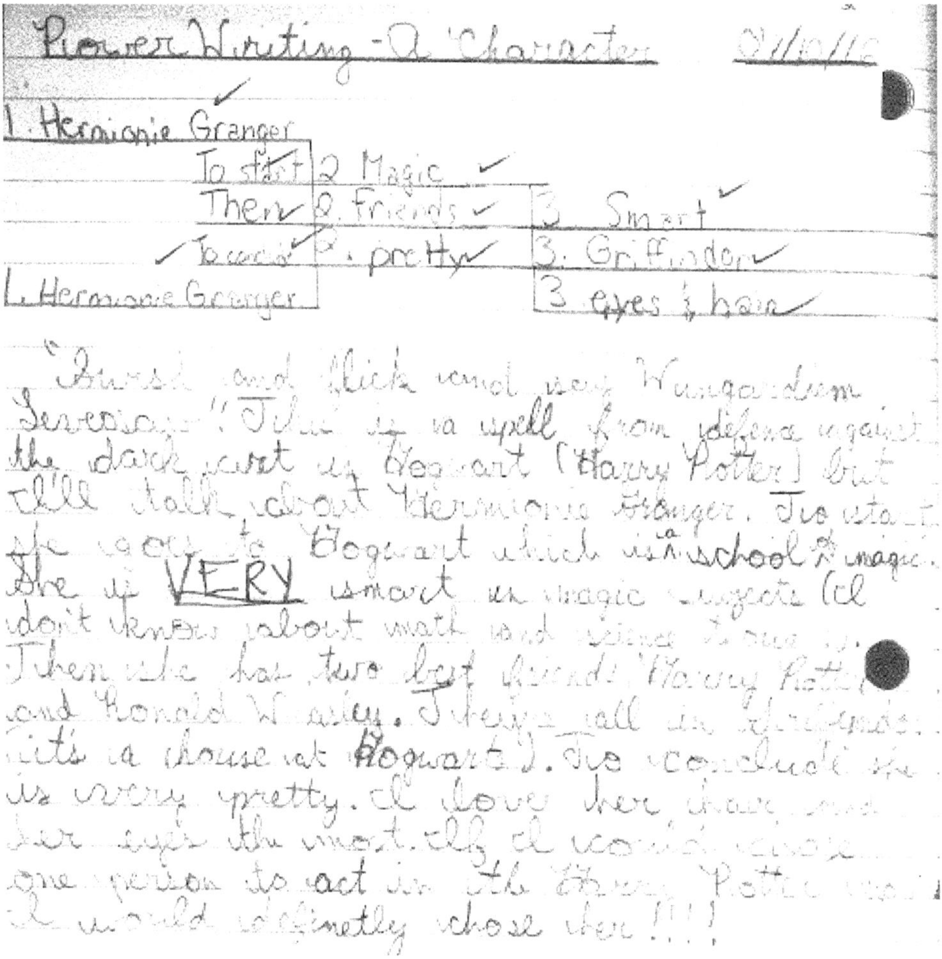
Power Writing - A Character

1. Hermionie Granger

To start 2. Magic

Then 2. Friends 3. Smart

To conclude 2. pretty 3. Griffindor

1. Hermionie Granger 3. eyes & hair

Transcribed:

“Swish and flick and say Wingardiem Leveosaw”. This is a spell from defence against the dark art in Hogwart (Harry Potter) but I’ll talk about Hermionie Granger. To start she goes to Hogwart which is a school of magic. She is <u>VERY</u> smart in magic subjects (I don’t know about math and science though). Then she has two best friends, Harry Potter and Ronald Weasley. They're all in Griffyndor (it's a house at Hogwarts). To conclude she is very pretty. I love her hair and her eyes the most. If I could chose one person to act in the Harry Potter movie I wold definitely chose her!!!!

Next Steps:

In this example, the student has taken time to organize her thoughts and demonstrates a well laid-out plan to write her paragraph. Note that checkmarks are visible on the graphic organizer indicating that she has included all ideas in her paragraph. This student has really captured the reader's attention through the Power 0 opener. The bracketed sentences and bolded/capitalized words demonstrates that the student is attempting to bring voice to her piece. Transition words follow the expectation. Next steps that a teacher may take with this student includes fine-tuning the Power 1. Currently, the Power 1 is not concisely stated to introduce that the paragraph will discuss the character, Hermione. A teacher may guide this student to choose more sophisticated transition words. Explicit teaching in the area of sentence fluency could be beneficial (e.g. how to integrate bracketed text as part of the flow of the sentence).

Example 6

Evaluated Level 3

My Top 5 Favourite Movies

Here are five of my favourite movies. First, I like watching "Pretty in Pink." This outstanding movie is about a poor girl who goes to the prom with a rich guy. Secondly, you should watch "Click." The main message in "Click" is that there are consequences for skipping stressful situations in life; you miss out on things. That's a great message. Also, I enjoy "Sweet Home Alabama." The point of this movie is to tell you that there are consequences for being someone you're not. In addition, the movie "Cars" is perfect for someone who is full of themselves. "Cars" has two messages: there's no 'I' in team, and it takes a team to win. Lastly, "High School Musical" is a spectacular movie. The movie is about a guy overcoming peer pressure. So, those are my 5 favourite movies.

Next Steps:

Although the graphic organizer is not included in this piece, the pattern (1, 2, 3, 2, 3, 2, 3, 2, 3, 2, 3, 1) is clearly evident. The title of the piece already indicates that the student would be discussing more than three powers of 2. Students should not feel limited to writing only three Power 2s in a given paragraph as long as the ideas interlink. The student has made conscious word choices that enhance the piece (e.g. outstanding, spectacular, consequences). Next steps may include improving the Power 1 sentences to make them more unique. Explicit teaching in various sentence starters may assist this student in escaping the usual pattern. Adding a Power 0 could add more intrigue to the piece.

Example 7

Evaluated Level 4

"Knock knock"
"Who's there"
"Man, I forgot, sorry".

Don't you just hate it when people waste your time to tell a joke, and they do a bad job telling it? Well, I'm going to tell you three things you shouldn't do when telling a joke. To start with, you should always remember it. If there's one thing I hate, it's when people forget the joke they're telling you. Tip number two, you should always use expression. If you talk like a robot people will feel like you just wasted their whole day. Finally, you should try not to tell the same joke to people over and over again. It makes them feel like yelling at you and running away. Try to use a variety of jokes. In conclusion, I hope you learned the wrong way to tell a joke, so that the next time you tell one, you make it interesting.

Next Steps:

The student has used an intriguing Power 0 introduction to not only grab the reader's attention but to add "voice". Note the excellent choice in transition in the second Power 2: "Tip number two…". This is quite sophisticated and innovative. Although the graphic organizer was not included, the paragraph's organizational structure clearly reveals the 1, 2, 3, 2, 3, 2, 3, 1 pattern. The student makes comparisons (simile) such as "…talk like a robot…" which also adds "voice". The author's humour is revealed with such lines as: "… makes them feel like yelling and running away". The student demonstrates excellent use of conventions such as quotations marks, commas, and no errors in spelling or punctuation. The next steps for this student may include further exploration of transition words and introduction to literary devices (i.e. metaphors, similes, personification, etc.). Further development of word choice could assist this student in maturing as a writer. The teacher may choose to model alternate ways to vary sentences to build the student's knowledge of sentence fluency.

Summary

The samples provided, written by real students, demonstrate the spectrum of ability of middle-schoolers. Remember that explicit teaching of the power writing process is key to your students' success in being able to generate ideas, organize and write a clear and concise paragraph. You will still model for this age group so that they can see how you include a variety of sentence lengths and more advanced word choices. Students in middle-school are especially creative with Power Zeros, even if they are mimicking what they hear in social settings or media exposure. Let them experiment and encourage them to explore their own voice. Guided writing and peer-editing is a great way to practise.

Once students have thoroughly grasped the power writing process and internalized the pattern to answer questions or communicate their understanding of a concept, you can progress to teaching them how to formulate a five-paragraph essay. Students at this age can handle more advanced concepts and begin to research various sources to brainstorm and organize facts. They move beyond their own feelings or ideas about a topic. The samples above demonstrate this as some explain their ideas about Native peoples of Canada. The next chapter will explain how to teach the structure of essay writing.

Part 3

From Paragraph to Essay

CHAPTER SIX

Power Writing Process for Essays

Non-fiction writing, especially reports or persuasive writing, is usually introduced in the middle-school grades. By secondary, students will have to write five-paragraph essays more regularly in various subjects. Some students may feel overwhelmed by the assignment and that is where the power writing process helps ease that anxiety. If a student is competent in writing a power paragraph of the 1-2-3-2-3-2-3-1 pattern, then they are ready to learn the structure of a five-paragraph essay. This chapter will guide you through the process of how to teach your students the pattern to generate ideas, organize points and write their essay.

Brainstorm and Research

As mentioned in previous chapters, brainstorming may seem like an easy activity, however, students really need guidance and modelling in order to determine which of the ideas connect well and would be worthy of choosing as a topic of interest. For this reason, teachers use various strategies to have their students recall information they already know and present new learning through various methods such as written text, multi-media, guest speakers, primary sources from archives and more. In the later grades of elementary, but especially in middle-school, students learn to synthesize information and connect similar ideas together. Once they learn to take information from reliable sources, properly credit the source and reword the ideas in their own words when not quoting directly, students will be able to organize their thoughts in a logical manner.

When students are making point-form notes on a topic, guide them to start thinking about three major details about the topic. They may wish to start organizing notes under Power 2s and then choose which three, Power 2s they want to expand on in the body of the essay. The next page illustrates the graphic organizer for a five-paragraph essay. Nothing changes from what you've taught students regarding a power paragraph. What expands is the first and fifth paragraphs are like the topic and concluding sentence from the paragraph format. In the topic paragraph the Power 2s each become a paragraph in the body of the essay.

Graphic Organizer

When teaching students to organize their facts or ideas for their essay, start with the 1-2-2-2-1 pattern. This will help them stay higher level and write a more concise essay. You can move towards a mix of paragraphs (i.e. some body paragraphs are 1-2-2-2-1 pattern and others may be 1-2-3-2-3-2-3-1 pattern) as a next step. Eventually, once students have internalized what a five-paragraph essay looks like, then Power Zero and the extended pattern will become the norm for them. This chapter deals with introducing students to the structure of the simplest form of the five-paragraph essay and therefore uses the 1-2-2-2-1 pattern. The essay structure is pictured below.

Graphic Organizer for Five-Paragraph Essay

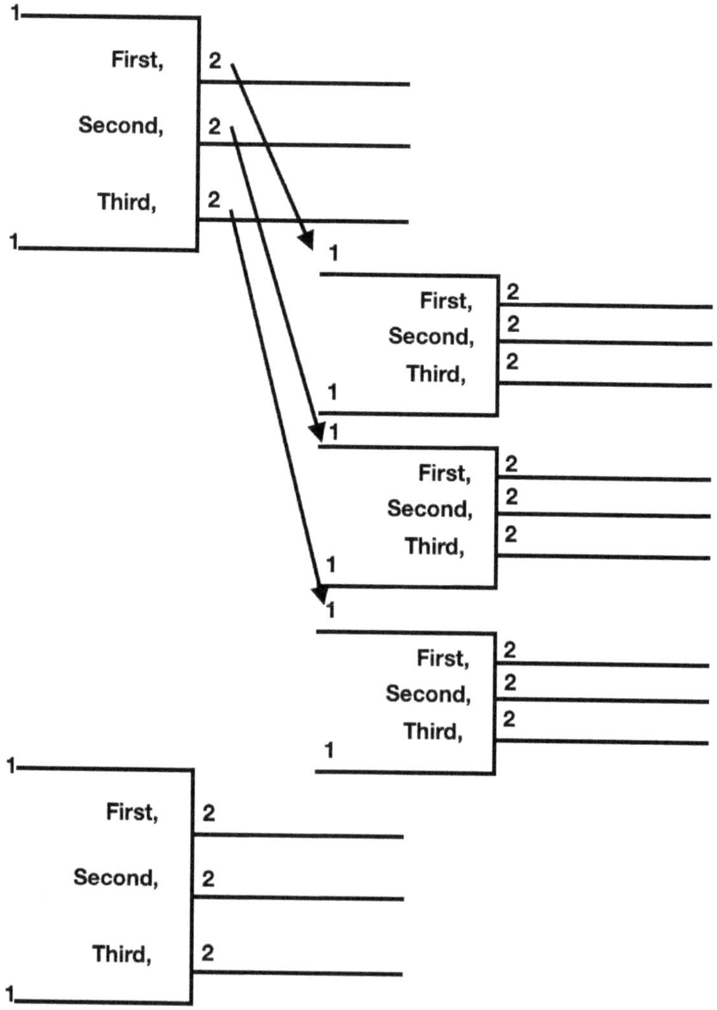

1
First, 2
Second, 2
Third, 2
1

1
First, 2
Second, 2
Third, 2
1

1
First, 2
Second, 2
Third, 2
1

1
First, 2
Second, 2
Third, 2
1

1
First, 2
Second, 2
Third, 2
1

Example Topic: Olympics

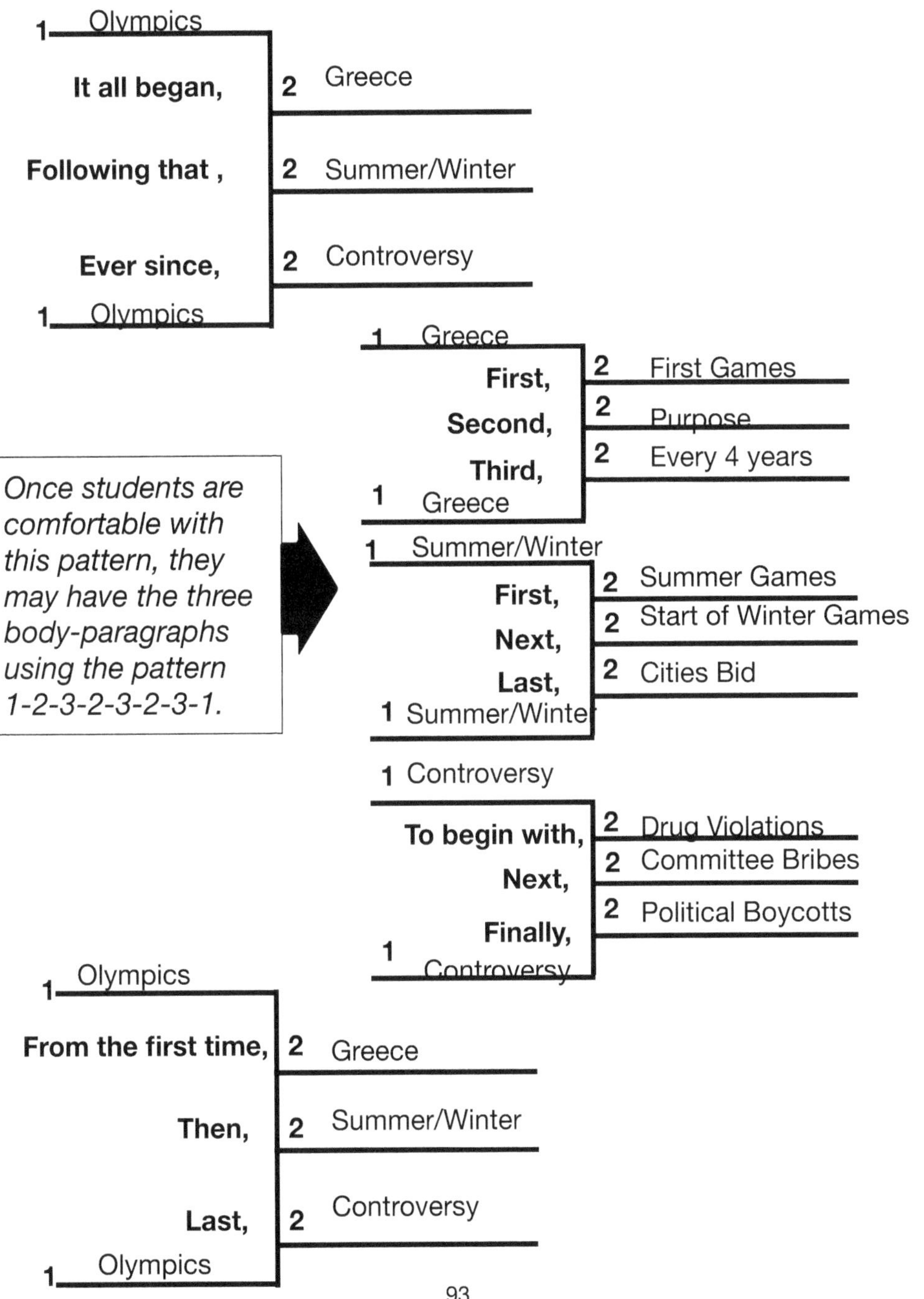

Example of Writing A First Draft Using the Graphic Organizer

Let's begin with the topic and concluding paragraphs to demonstrate how the graphic organizer helps the student write the topic and concluding paragraphs first.

Topic Paragraph

Power Zero:

After all the sweat, tears and physical exertion, you can taste gold!

Transition Words:
It all began
Following that
Ever since
Yet

After all the sweat, tears and physical exertion, you can taste gold!

P1: Welcome to the Olympic Games that started in Greece, have expanded to become summer and winter games and, have had its fair share of controversies.

P1: Yet, the Olympics remain a popular, global endeavour where nations compete and demonstrate athletic excellence.

P2: It all began in Greece where the games were a friendly gathering of locals to demonstrate their athletic excellence.

P2: Following that, in the early twentieth century the Winter Olympic Games were added to the Summer range of sports and athletic endeavours.

P2: Ever since then there have been controversies that have at times blemished the Olympic Games.

Concluding Paragraph

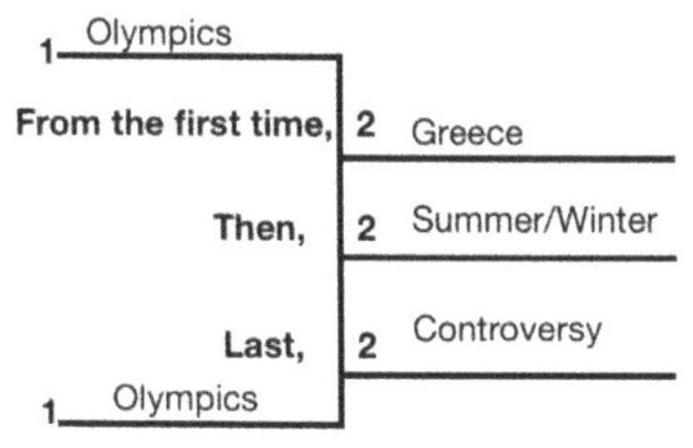

Transition Words:
In conclusion,
From the first time,
Then
Last,
All in All

P1: In conclusion, participating as an athlete, let alone winning a medal at the Olympics is an amazing experience.

P1: All in all, the purpose of the original Olympics, the fierce competition between nations in both the summer and winter games and, the joy of winning medals overrides the controversies that sometimes mar the Olympic Games.

P2: From the first time the games were held in Olympia to honour Zeus, the tradition has carried on for many centuries.

P2: Then, in the modern era, the Olympics have expanded and divided into summer and winter games, with many new sports added to the list of competitions.

P2: Last, the Olympics are not without its controversies which includes athletes who have violated rules, the Olympic Committee fraught with bribes and, political boycotts that see certain countries bowing out.

Now that the student has drafted the topic and concluding paragraphs, they are ready to move to the body paragraphs. The reason you would coach students to write the topic and concluding paragraphs first is because they are virtually the same paragraph with some changes in the wording of the sentences. For many students it is easier when they are looking at the big picture before they move on to the details. Remember this is a first draft, so where a student may be missing transition words or their topic sentence isn't quite on the mark, teachers would coach and provide feedback related to the criteria established in the rubric.

First Body Paragraph

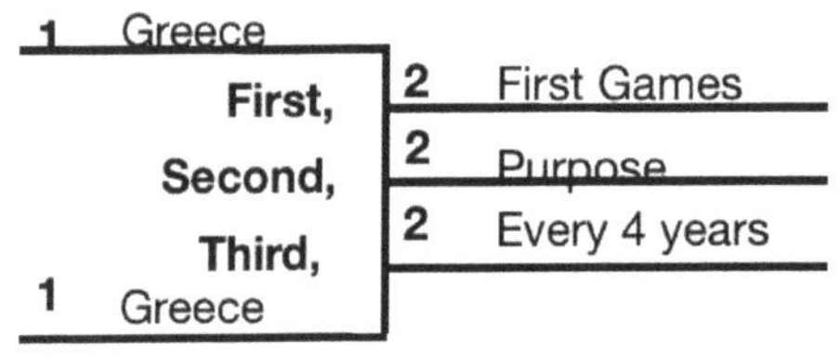

Transition Words:
Although

P1: The Olympic Games originated in Greece.

P1: It is really wonderful that Greece is still honoured as the birthplace of the Olympics.

P2: Some 700 years before the current epoch, the first Olympic Games were held (reference).

P2: They were held in Olympia in honour of Zeus, the sky and thunder god (reference).

P2: Although it is unclear why they were held every four years, it became the measure of time and usually a truce between waring parties occurred.

Second Body Paragraph

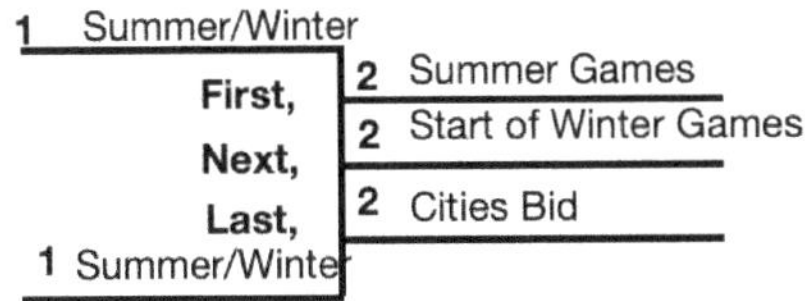

Transition Words:
First,
Next,
Last,

P1: Now a days we are familiar with both the Summer and Winter Olympic Games as a global competition.

P1: The global competition between athletes from countries all over the word participating in various winter and summer sports is an exciting event.

P2: First, the modern version of the Summer Games began in 1896 and were held in Athens (reference).

P2: Next, the Winter Games began in 1924 but in 1994 they ceased being held the same year as the Summer Games (reference).

P2: Last, it is fierce competition between cities who bid to host the Olympic Games many years before they are to be held.

Remember, these paragraphs were constructed by first writing the P1 sentences. Read it that way to get the feel for how the student would have written it. Then read the P2 sentences individually and see if it connects back to the idea on the graphic organizer. That is the thinking process the student goes through in drafting the paragraphs.

Third Body Paragraph

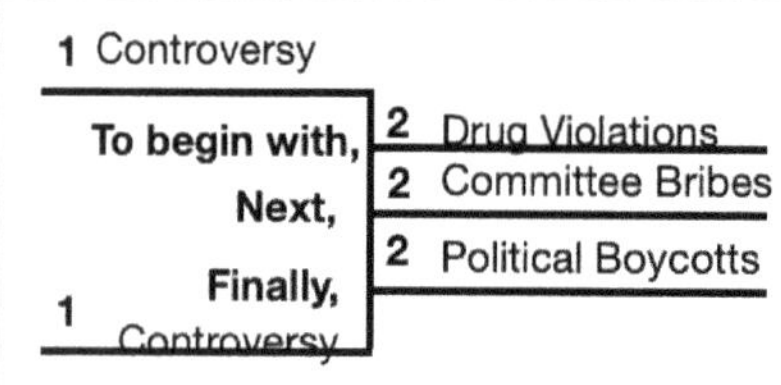 Transition Words: To begin with, Next, Finally,	P1: There have been controversies such as drug violations, committee bribes and political boycotts in modern times. P1: These are just three examples of controversies that have affected the Olympic Games. P2: To begin with, athletes compete at the highest level and sometimes the pressure has them make mistakes, like taking illegal substances to enhance their performance. P2: Next, you may have heard in the media about committee bribes when cities are trying to secure their Olympic bid. P2: Finally, the most famous political boycott occurred in 1980 when Russia hosted the games and the USA refused to participate due to Russia invading Afghanistan (reference).

Putting it All Together

The student is now ready to write the first draft having constructed the sentences for the topic and concluding paragraphs as well as the three, body paragraphs. Remember that once a first draft is written, the student will go back to the rubric or checklist to ensure they are meeting the criteria. This is a good opportunity for self-evaluation before peer-editing. Teachers would provide feedback on the graphic organizer ideas, have the student orally rehearse what they'll say about the idea and then make sure they are following their graphic organizer so they stay on topic. What follows is the draft essay in chronological flow. As you read it, think of what feedback you would provide based on the rubric from previous chapters.

Example Draft Essay: Olympics

After all the sweat, tears and physical exertion, you can taste gold! Welcome to the Olympic Games that started in Greece, have expanded to become summer and winter games and, have had its fair share of controversies. It all began in Greece where the games were a friendly gathering of locals to demonstrate their athletic excellence. Following that, in the early twentieth century the Winter Olympic Games were added to the Summer range of sports and athletic endeavours. Ever since then there have been controversies that have at times blemished the Olympic Games. Yet, the Olympics remain a popular, global endeavour where nations compete and demonstrate athletic excellence.

The Olympic Games originated in Greece. Some 700 years before the current epoch, the first Olympic Games were held (reference). They were held in Olympia in honour of Zeus, the sky and thunder god (reference). Although it is unclear why they were held every four years, it became the measure of time and usually a truce between waring parties occurred. It is really wonderful that Greece is still honoured as the birthplace of the Olympics.

Now a days we are familiar with both the Summer and Winter Olympic Games as a global competition. First, the modern version of the Summer Games began in 1896 and were held in Athens (reference). Next, the Winter Games began in 1924 but in 1994 they ceased being held the same year as the Summer Games (reference). Last, it is fierce competition between cities who bid to host the Olympic Games many years before they are to be held. The global competition between athletes from countries all over the word participating in various winter and summer sports is an exciting event.

There have been controversies such as drug violations, committee bribes and political boycotts in modern times. To begin with, athletes compete at the highest level and sometimes the pressure has them make mistakes, like taking illegal substances to enhance their performance. Next, you may have heard in the media about committee bribes when cities are trying to secure their Olympic bid. Finally, the most famous political boycott occurred in 1980 when Russia hosted the games and the USA refused to participate due to Russia invading Afghanistan (reference). These are just three examples of controversies that have affected the Olympic Games.

In conclusion, participating as an athlete, let alone winning a medal at the Olympics is an amazing experience. From the first time the games were held in Olympia to honour Zeus, the tradition has carried on for many centuries. In the modern era, the Olympics have expanded and divided into summer and winter games, with many new sports added to the list of competitions. Last, the Olympics are not without its controversies which includes athletes who have violated rules, the Olympic Committee fraught with bribes and, political boycotts that see certain countries bowing out. All in all, the purpose of the original Olympics, the fierce competition between nations in both the summer and winter games and, the joy of winning medals overrides the controversies that sometimes mar the Olympic Games.

Summary

Breaking down the overwhelming task of writing an essay will provide students with confidence in their ability to complete the assignment. It is really important that students have a sound grasp of how to construct a paragraph using the Power Writing process. Start with the 1-2-2-2-1 pattern when they first have to write an essay. Some of your students may actually include some 1-2-3-2-3-2-3-1 paragraphs, which is great, but it is important to ensure it actually is the correct pattern and not add-ons that are not connected to the major idea (Power 2). Using a clear criteria checklist or rubric will help students self-assess and make them more accountable for meeting the expectations outlined. Provide clear and direct feedback to help students improve. This can be as simple as having them search for better transition words or using a variety of sentence lengths if they are always writing short sentences. Don't underestimate the amount of modelling and practise required. Eventually as the school year progresses, all you'll need to say is "write a power paragraph about..." and students will know exactly what to do. It is one of those skills that they will use throughout their lifetime.

Part 4

Appendices

Appendix 1 - Brainstorming Teaching Strategies

In chapter one several teaching strategies were mentioned to help with brainstorming and generating ideas. A brief explanation is provided below.

Think-Pair-Share

Students shouldn't work in isolation when we are first learning to express ourselves through written text. An effective and collaborative brainstorming strategy is Think-Pair-Share. First have students **think** to themselves for a set amount of time appropriate for their age. A good rule of thumb is 30 seconds for younger students and up to a minute for older students. Encourage quiet reflection, students can put their heads-down, they may even scribble if they wish. The point here is not to speak with others until it's time to **pair**. Once time has elapsed, you can either partner the students or have them pair with their elbow buddy (someone closest to them). Set a time and signal for them to share with their partners the ideas or answers they come up with related to the topic or question you have posed. After that time elapses, it is time to **share** with the entire class. Signal the students to focus on the front. You now know that even students who may not have had ideas on their own can safely offer ideas from what they talked about in their pairing. Need more guidance, go to: https://tinyurl.com/yuy3ksdj

KWL

This acronym stands for know, want-to-know, and learned. Create a three-column chart and write the letters as the title for each column (you can add the words if the students aren't familiar with what they mean). When you want to brainstorm with the students, start with what they already know about the subject. Add their contributions to the first column. The second column lists the students' wonderings, what they want to know about the topic, or something that they aren't sure about and need to verify. Leave the third column for the end of the lesson (or unit) once students can contribute what they have learned.

Whole-Class Brainstorm

Some basic rules about whole-class brainstorming are:

- Accept all answers (even if you know they are wrong or not related to the topic, be strategic and place them somewhere less prominent on your diagram)
- Try to solicit as many ideas as possible ensuring quiet voices are also heard
- Remain neutral when receiving suggestions
- Signal that you will conclude the brainstorming after three more suggestions (or whatever number you wish).

After the brainstorming has concluded, guide the class in determining which ideas/words are similar and could be grouped together. Seek clarification from students regarding words/ideas you aren't sure of how they relate to the topic.

Minds-On

The strategy is "hands-on, minds-on" where students engage in active learning. Here students physically move to grasp a concept. If you are going to brainstorm with younger students about, for example elephants, it helps them to move around the room, using all their sense to get their minds-on how elephants move, communicate, interact and what sounds they make. You can read a storybook about elephants so students get their minds-on the topic. You can also show a video related to the topic. Once the students have their minds-on the topic they are ready to brainstorm ideas.

Appendix 2 - Transition Words

The brief list of transition words provided in chapter one is a great start to consistently use when first teaching students the Power Writing process. Once students are independent in constructing the advanced pattern (0-1-2-3-2-3-2-3-1) with confidence, teachers will coach them to begin experimenting with alternative transition words. Here is a more elaborate list.

First	Second	Third
In the first place	Next	In addition (to this)
To begin with	Subsequently	As well (as this)
To start with	Then	What is more
Initially	Further(more)	Besides
For the purpose of	On the other hand	Above all
Foremost	Not only (this)	But also (that) as well
Primarily	However	But even so
Basically	Succeeding	On a final note
First thing	Furthermore	In winding up
In advance of	Similarly	In time

First	Second	Third
Originally	In contrast	While
Before all else	Nonetheless	Nevertheless
Beforehand	Although	(And) still
First off	(And) yet	In either case
In the beginning	However	Either way
Originally	Whichever/Whatever happens	As a result
The earliest	As was previously stated	To conclude with
Immediately	Thus	Last but not least
Up front	Incidentally	Eventually
Generally	After this	In short / in sum
Especially	Less important	To finish
Preeminently	Supplementary	To bring to an end
Prevalently	Another point	In closing / In conclusion
Notably	Following	To wind up
Particularly	Directly after	In summary
Notably	Next in order	Last but not least
Important to note	After the first	On the whole
For the most part	Supporting	Ultimately
The main reason	Later	Overall
Essentially	Second of the (two, three)	Taking everything into account
As an introduction	Also	Succinctly

Appendix 3 - Interesting Adjectives and Exciting Verbs

Students typically use the basic adjectives and verbs repetitively in their writing until they are exposed to texts that include a variety of adjectives and verbs. However, teachers should model, explicitly teach and, provide feedback for repetitive usage of adjectives like "nice" and verbs like "get" and "said". The following lists are meant as a starting point that you can post in your classroom and add on to as your students expand their vocabularies.

Interesting Adjectives

Nice	**Big**	**Fun**
Amusing	Considerable	Witty
Enjoyable	Enormous	Charming
Likable	Huge	Delightful
Kind	Immense	Hilarious
Pleasant	Large	Entertaining

Nice	Big	Fun
Agreeable	Sizeable	Amusing
Delightful	Substantial	Pleasing

Pretty	Gross	Small
Charming	Flagrant	Little
Attractive	Blatant	Small-scale
Lovely	Disgusting	Compact
Good/Nice-looking	Revolting	Portable
Fetching	Repellent	Tiny
Appealing	Repulsive	Miniature / mini
Delightful	Sickening	Microscopic
Glamrous	Nauseating	Itty-bitty / teeny-weeny / teensy
Cute	Off-putting	Puny

Exciting Verbs

Went	Look	Walk
Set off / out	Peer	Amble
Leave	Gaze	Saunter
Take one's leave	Gawk	Stroll
Retire	Stare	Wander
Withdraw	Inspect	Stride

Went	Look	Walk
Hightail it	Consider	Gallop
Scoot	Scrutinize	Skip
Run away /off	View	Waddle
Retreat	Glance	Slither

Play	Have	Go
Amuse / Entertain / Enjoy oneself	Possess / Be in possession of	Make one's way
Participate	Own	Proceed
Engage in	Occupy	Move
Be involved in	Utilize	Progress
Join / Compete in	Keep	Pass
Act / Enact	Maintain	Walk
Portray / Represent	Retain	Travel
Pretend to be	Hold	Journey
Active	Contain	Depart

Said / Say / Tell	Get	Excited
Declare	Gain	Stimulate
State	Earn	Electrify
Announce	Take possession of	Delight
Remark	Collect	Pep up
Mention	Grab	Rouse

Said / Say / Tell	Get	Excited
Speak	Acquire	Thrill
Utter	Obtain	Exhilarate
Voice	Come to have	Animate
Pronounce	Receive	Stir (up)

Appendix 4 - Downloadable Templates

The following pages provide you with reproducible templates of the graphic organizers and rubrics. The links allow you to download the templates so you can tailor them for your classroom use.

Remember the teacher version of the rubric is meant to make your assessment of students' writing assignments easier and faster. Yes, you will still read through their work but you know exactly what to look for. You can simplify, depending on age/grade of the students your 'teacher' rubric so that students can use it for self-assessment and peer-evaluation. This increases their accountability and focus.

Last, teacher-moderation is one of the most rewarding professional experiences, in my opinion. With a grade-partner see if you can coordinate your planning time and work smarter not harder by marking together. It will allow you to use the communal rubric and be more objective when evaluating the work of the other students.

Name:_______________

____

____

____

Name:______________ Date: ______________

1

First, 2

Second, 2

Third, 2

1

Name:______________ Date: ______________

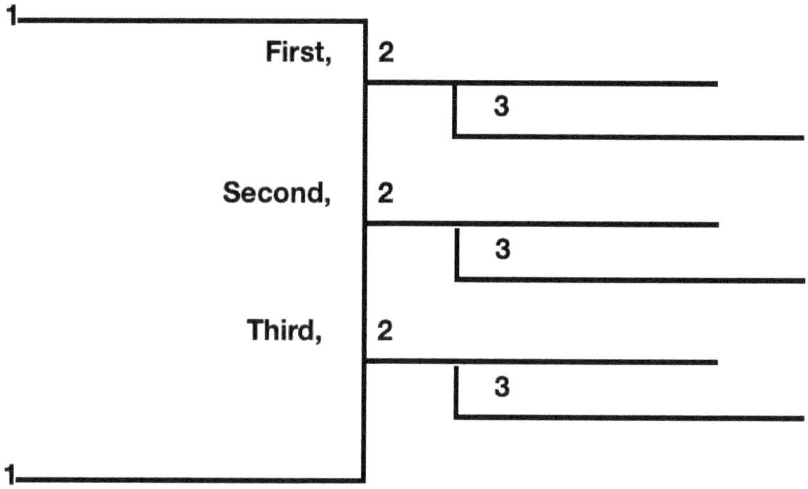

1

First, 2

3

Second, 2

3

Third, 2

3

1

Name:______________ Date: ______________

ZERO

1

First, 2

3

Second, 2

3

Third, 2

3

1

Name:____________ Date: ____________

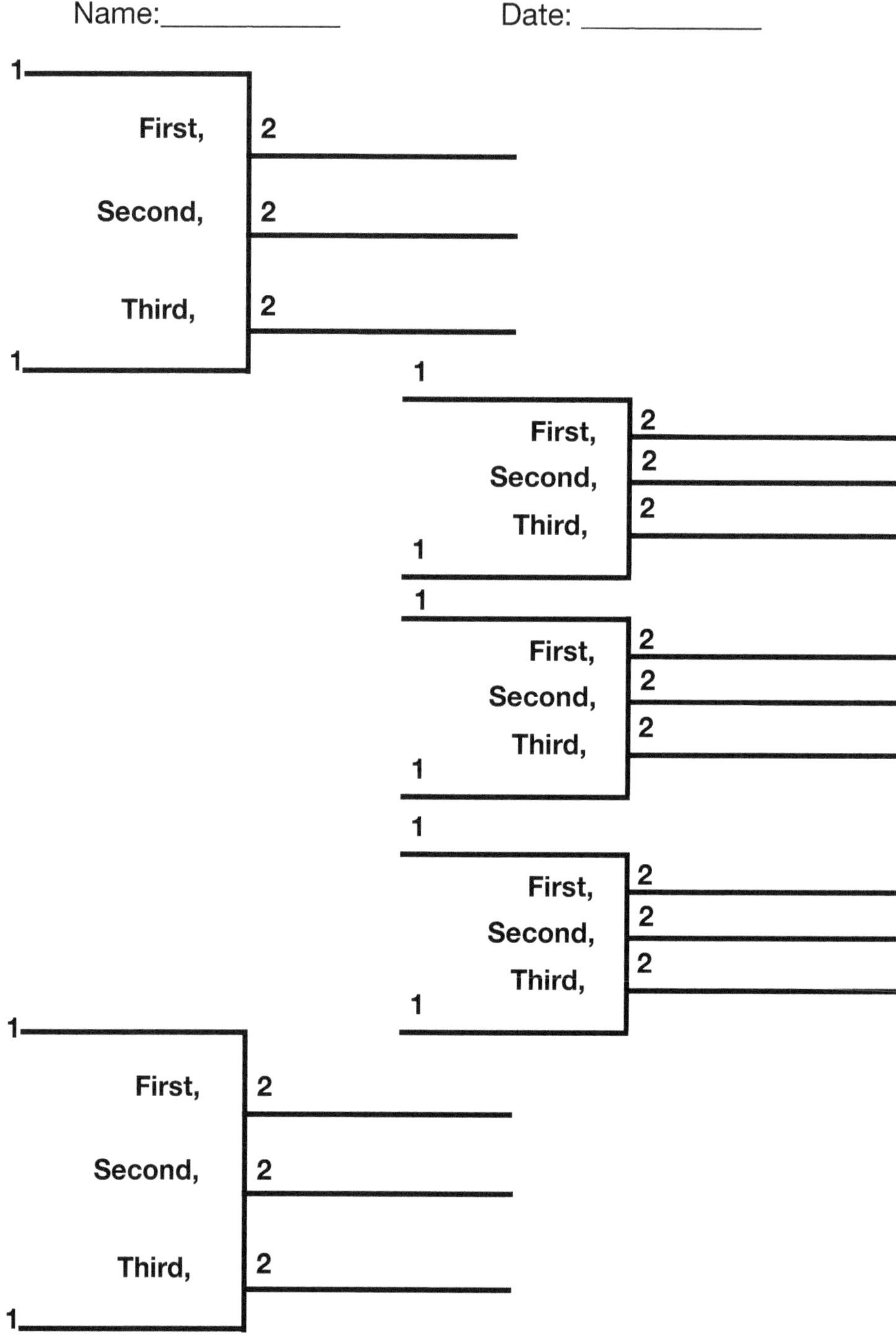
1
First,
2
Second,
2
Third,
2
1
1
First,
2
Second,
2
Third,
2
1
1
First,
2
Second,
2
Third,
2
1
1
First,
2
Second,
2
Third,
2
1
1
First,
2
Second,
2
Third,
2
1

For the listed graphic organizers or to modify them (e.g. change the transition words) follow the link below.

Graphic Organizer - Kindergarten

Graphic Organizer - Pattern 1-2-2-2-1

Graphic Organizer - Pattern 1-2-3-2-3-2-3-1

Graphic Organizer - Pattern 0-1-2-3-2-3-2-3-1

Graphic Organizer - Essay

https://forms.gle/5Ksoy3hVm5TZihxM8

Kindergarten Power Writing Checklist (for Teachers)

Student has demonstrated growth in the use of: *(highlight or checkmark applicable criteria)*

Ideas

- ☐ Follows modelled organizer
- ☐ Generates their own ideas for writing

Power Writing Format

- ☐ Opening sentence
- ☐ Closing sentence
- ☐ 3 supporting/related details

Word Choice

- ☐ Incorporated theme or modelled words
- ☐ Use of synonyms "Fancy Words" *(e.g. huge vs big)*
- ☐ Use of descriptive language

Attitudes

- ☐ Evidence of risk taking in their writing
- ☐ Willingness to undertake the writing task
- ☐ Understanding that their writing communicates a message
- ☐ Evidence of pride in their finish product
- ☐ Positively responds to feedback

Spelling

- ☐ Initial sounds only
- ☐ Initial and end sounds
- ☐ Phonetically recognizable words (without vowels)
- ☐ Phonetically recognizable words (with vowels)
- ☐ High frequency words spelled correctly as specified by the teacher
- ☐ Use of environmental print (e.g. classroom resources)

Conventions

- ☐ Capitals
- ☐ Spaces
- ☐ Punctuation
- ☐ Proper use of upper/lower case letters
- ☐ Left to right progression
- ☐ Correct letter orientation

Anecdotal Notes:

Name:______________ Date: ______________

I used 

I wrote 

opening

I wrote 

closing

I used 

I used  “fancy words”

Categories	Expectations	Level 4	Level 3	Level 2	Level 1
Graphic Organizer **IDEAS**	Organizer is followed to generate introduction and supporting ideas	Details connect **specifically** to the main idea. Details are purposefully linked. The graphic organizer is thoughtful and focused.	Details connect **directly** to the main idea. There is a clear link between the details.	Details connect to the main idea. The relationship between the ideas are unclear or the ideas don't match.	Includes main idea. Details lack connection to the main idea.
	Power 1 and 2 *Here you would include examples of the topic*	Pets Kitten Puppy Hamster Pets	Animals Kitten Puppy Cub Animals	Animals Kitten Bear Furry Animals	Animals Love them Eat Zoo Animals
	Power 1, 2 and 3 (after mastering Power 1 and 2) *Here you would include examples of the topic*	Pets Kitten Claws at fishbowl Puppy Chews socks Hamster Burrows a nest Pets	Pets Kitten Purs & meows Puppy Licks face Cub Runs in wheel Pets	Pets Kitten Muffin Bear Small Furry Eats pellets Pets	Pets Kitten Puppy Brown Hamster No Pets
Power 1 **ORGANIZATION**	Main Idea - topic sentence refers to first and last sentence	Topic sentences are **exceptionally clear** and connected to the main idea.	Topic sentences are **well stated**. The last sentence is linked to the main idea (or vice-versa)	Topic sentence is **clear**. The last sentence does not relate back to the main idea (or vice-versa).	Topic and/or last sentence is **unclear.** There is no topic/last sentence. Not sure what the main idea is.
Power 2	Major Details	Paragraph has **three** detail sentences which **strongly** connect to the main idea.	Paragraph has **three** supporting detail sentences which **relate well** to the main idea.	Paragraph has minimum **two** supporting detail sentences which relate somewhat back to the main idea.	Paragraph has **one** supporting detail sentence which attempts to relate back to the main idea.
Power 3	Minor Details connecting to Power 2	Paragraph has **three or more** detail sentences which **strongly and clearly** connect to *Power 2*. The sentences flow like you're talking.	Paragraph has **three** detail sentences that each extend upon *Power 2*. The sentences flow one to another and ideas are mostly connected.	Paragraph has minimum **two** detail sentences that extend upon a *Power 2*. The ideas between Power 2s and Power 3s are not always connected.	Paragraph has **one or more** detail sentences but the ideas do not connect to the *Power 2*.

1 of 2

Categories	Expectations	Level 4	Level 3	Level 2	Level 1
Power 0 **V O**	Catchy phrase or hook linked to the topic sentence.	The hook "wows" the reader (i.e. makes them laugh, respond, question etc.). Connects perfectly with the paragraph.	The hook grabs the reader's attention and fits well with the paragraph.	The hook fits but needs to be more specific to the topic.	The hook seems out of place and is not effective. It does not grab the reader's attention for the right reasons.
Voice **I C E**	My personal mark is left.	Uses two or more of the following: Questions, sound words, human characteristics to non-human things or similes.	The paragraph asks questions, or uses sound words, or gives human characteristics to non-human things or uses "like" or "as" to compare two things.	Attempts to use questions or sound words (e.g. snap, buzz, pop) to bring their personal feeling into their writing.	No attempt to use questions or sound words.
Fluency	The smoothness and flow of the written piece.	It is easy to read the sentences aloud. Sentence beginnings are interesting and varied. The sentences are different lengths.	Sentences are well built. It is easy to read the sentences aloud. Sentence beginnings are interesting. The sentences are different lengths.	There are some places to make smoother when I read aloud. Attempts to begin sentences in different ways. Blend or separate some sentences to make the different lengths	The sentences aren't working well. It is difficult to read the paragraph aloud as it needs to be smoother. The beginnings all sound the same. Too much use of "*and*".
Word Choice	Effective word choice.	Word choice includes **exceptional** transition words, a variety of descriptive and action words. A vivid picture is created for the reader.	Word choice includes various transition, descriptive and action words. Creates a clear picture for the reader.	Word choice is **adequate** because it adds only a bit of details. Uses familiar transition words. The reader begins to create a picture in their mind.	Word choice is **simple** and **repetitive**. Uses modelled transition words (e.g. Firstly, Secondly, Thirdly). The reader has a difficult time painting a picture in their mind.
Conventions	Mechanics are correct.	Paragraph has no punctuation, capitalization, grammar and spelling errors.	Paragraph has **very few** punctuation, capitalization, grammar and spelling errors.	Paragraph has **several** punctuation, capitalization, grammar and spelling errors.	Paragraph has **many** punctuation, capitalization, grammar and spelling errors.

Elementary Student Rubric

Categories	Expectations	Level 4	Level 3	Level 2	Level 1
Graphic Organizer	My organizer is complete	I have checked with 3 or more friends that my Graphic Organizer is correct.	I have checked with 2 friends that my Graphic Organizer is correct.	I have checked with one friend that my Graphic Organizer is correct	I completed my Graphic Organizer but have some errors.
If pattern 1-2-2-2-1 is assigned keep this row and delete the next or vice-versa.	Power 1 and 2 *Here you would include examples of the topic*	Pets Kitten Puppy Hamster Pets	Animals Kitten Puppy Cub Animals	Animals Kitten Bear Furry Animals	Animals Love them Eat Zoo Animals
	Power 1, 2 and 3 (after mastering Power 1 and 2) *Here you would include examples of the topic*	Pets Kitten Claws at fishbowl Puppy Chews socks Hamster Burrows a nest Pets	Pets Kitten Purs & meows Puppy Licks face Cub Runs in wheel Pets	Pets Kitten Muffin Bear Small Furry Eats pellets Pets	Pets Kitten Puppy Brown Hamster No Pets
Power 1 **Power 2** **[Power 3]** **Sentences**	I have a topic (opening & closing) sentence. I have three, detail sentences. [I have three minor detail sentences for each P2 sentence]	I have a **really great** opening & closing sentence. I have **three** detail sentences. I **know** my sentences make sense.	I have a **good** opening & closing sentence. I have **three** detail sentences. I **think** most of my sentences make sense.	I have an opening & closing sentence. I have at least **two** detail sentences. There may be one or two sentences that are **kind of confusing**.	I **think** I have an opening & closing sentence. I **tried** to write detail sentences. When I read the paragraph it's a bit (or a lot) **confusing**.
	I have checked the smoothness and flow of my paragraph	It is **easy, and smooth,** when my teacher/friend reads my paragraph aloud.	It is **easy** for my friend/ teacher to read the sentences aloud.	Sometimes my teacher/ friend **stumbles** when they read my sentences aloud.	It is difficult for my friend/ teacher to read the paragraph aloud as it has **words mixed up**.
Conventions	I have checked my conventions	I checked my spelling, punctuation and verb agreements. There are **no mistakes**.	I checked my spelling, punctuation and verb agreements. There are **one or two** mistakes.	I checked my spelling, punctuation and verb agreements. There are **several** mistakes.	I checked my spelling, punctuation and verb agreements. There are **a lot** of mistakes.

Middle-School Student Rubric

Categories	Expectations	Level 4	Level 3	Level 2	Level 1
Graphic Organizer	My organizer is complete	I have my Power 1 topic word written. I have three details that connect really well together.	I have my Power 1 topic word written. I have three details that I think connect.	I have my Power 1 topic word written. I have three details but I'm not sure how well they connect.	I have my Power 1 topic word written. I have three details but they don't all match.
If pattern 1-2-2-2-1 is assigned keep this row and delete the next or vice-versa.	Power 1 and 2 *Here you would include examples of the topic*	Pets Kitten Puppy Hamster Pets	Animals Kitten Puppy Cub Animals	Animals Kitten Bear Furry Animals	Animals Love them Eat Zoo Animals
	Power 1, 2 and 3 (after mastering Power 1 and 2) *Here you would include examples of the topic*	Pets Kitten Claws at fishbowl Puppy Chews socks Hamster Burrows a nest Pets	Pets Kitten Purs & meows Puppy Licks face Cub Runs in wheel Pets	Pets Kitten Muffin Bear Small Furry Eats pellets Pets	Pets Kitten Puppy Brown Hamster No Pets
Power 1 Power 2 [Power 3] Sentences	I have a topic (opening & closing) sentence. I have three, detail sentences. [I have three, minor detail sentences that connect well to each P2 sentence]	Topic sentences are **exceptionally clear**. The **three** detail sentences connect **strongly** to main idea.	Topic sentences are **well written directly connect.** The **three** detail sentences connect **relate well** to main idea. There are improvements I can make in word choice or sentence length.	Topic sentence is **clear**. Paragraph has minimum **two** supporting detail sentences which relate **somewhat** back to the main idea. There are **several** improvements I can make.	Topic and/or last sentence is **unclear.** Paragraph has at least **one** supporting detail sentence but when I read it, it is a bit confusing. I can make more improvements to make it sound better.
	The smoothness and flow of the written piece.	It is **easy, and smooth,** to read the sentences aloud. The sentences are different lengths.	It is easy to read the sentences aloud. Some sentences are different lengths.	Some **stumbles** when I read the sentences aloud. Many of my sentences start the same way & same length.	It is difficult to read the paragraph aloud as it has words mixed up. Most of the sentences sound the same or use "and" too much.
Conventions	Mechanics are correct.	Paragraph has no punctuation, capitalization, grammar and spelling errors.	Paragraph has **very few** punctuation, capitalization, grammar and spelling errors.	Paragraph has **several** punctuation, capitalization, grammar and spelling errors.	Paragraph has **many** punctuation, capitalization, grammar and spelling errors.

Essay Rubric

Categories	Expectations	Level 4	Level 3	Level 2	Level 1
Graphic Organizer	Organizer is followed to generate introduction and supporting ideas	Details connect **specifically** to the main idea. Details are purposefully linked. The graphic organizer is thoughtful and focused.	Details connect **directly** to the main idea. There is a clear link between the details.	Details connect to the main idea. The relationship between the ideas are unclear or the ideas don't match.	Includes main idea. Details lack connection to the main idea.
Essay Structure	There is a clear opening and closing paragraph that follows the graphic organizer.	Topic paragraphs are **exceptionally clear**. The **three** detail sentences connect **strongly** to main idea.	Topic paragraphs are **direct and clear**. The **three** detail sentences connect **well** to main idea.	Topic paragraphs are **somewhat clear**. The **three** detail sentences connect **mostly** to main idea.	Topic paragraphs are **confusing or unclear**. The **three** detail sentences **diverge from** the main idea.
	The three body-paragraphs elaborate on each of the Power 2 major details from the opening paragraph.	Each of three paragraphs are **exceptionally clear**. It is **very clear** how each paragraph connects back to the opening and closing paragraph P2s (P3s).	Each of three paragraphs are **clear**. It is **clear** how each paragraph connects back to the opening and closing paragraph P2s (P3s).	Each of three paragraphs are **present**. Some of the paragraphs are missing some connection back to the opening and closing paragraph P2s (P3s).	There is an **attempt to follow the structure**. The details in one or more paragraph differ from, or do not directly connect back to, the opening & closing paragraph.
	All essay paragraphs are evaluated and the most consistent performance is checked/highlighted below.				
Power 1	Main Idea - topic sentence refers to first and last sentence	Topic sentences are **exceptionally clear** and connected to the main idea.	Topic sentences are **well stated**. The last sentence is linked to the main idea (or vice-versa)	Topic sentence is **clear**. The last sentence does not relate back to the main idea (or vice-versa).	Topic and/or last sentence is **unclear.** There is no topic/last sentence. Not sure what the main idea is.
Power 2	Major Details	Paragraph has **three** detail sentences which **strongly** connect to the main idea.	Paragraph has **three** supporting detail sentences which **relate well** to the main idea.	Paragraph has minimum **two** supporting detail sentences which relate somewhat back to the main idea.	Paragraph has **one** supporting detail sentence which attempts to relate back to the main idea.
Power 3	Minor Details connecting to Power 2	Paragraph has **three or more** detail sentences which **strongly and clearly** connect to *Power 2*. The sentences flow like you're talking.	Paragraph has **three** detail sentences that each extend upon *Power 2*. The sentences flow one to another and ideas are mostly connected.	Paragraph has minimum **two** detail sentences that extend upon a *Power 2*. The ideas between Power 2s and Power 3s are not always connected.	Paragraph has **one or more** detail sentences but the ideas do not connect to the *Power 2*.

Categories	Expectations	Level 4	Level 3	Level 2	Level 1
Power 0	Catchy phrase or hook linked to the topic sentence.	The hook "wows" the reader (i.e. makes them laugh, respond, question etc.). Connects perfectly with the paragraph.	The hook grabs the reader's attention and fits well with the paragraph.	The hook fits but needs to be more specific to the topic.	The hook seems out of place and is not effective. It does not grab the reader's attention for the right reasons.
Voice	My personal mark is left.	Uses two or more of the following: Questions, sound words, human characteristics to non-human things or similes.	The paragraph asks questions, or uses sound words, or gives human characteristics to non-human things or uses "like" or "as" to compare two things.	Attempts to use questions or sound words (e.g. snap, buzz, pop) to bring their personal feeling into their writing.	No attempt to use questions or sound words.
Fluency	The smoothness and flow of the written piece.	It is easy to read the sentences aloud. Sentence beginnings are interesting and varied. The sentences are different lengths.	Sentences are well built. It is easy to read the sentences aloud. Sentence beginnings are interesting. The sentences are different lengths.	There are some places to make smoother when I read aloud. Attempts to begin sentences in different ways. Blend or separate some sentences to make the different lengths	The sentences aren't working well. It is difficult to read the paragraph aloud as it needs to be smoother. The beginnings all sound the same. Too much use of "*and*".
Word Choice	Effective word choice.	Word choice includes **exceptional** transition words, a variety of descriptive and action words. A vivid picture is created for the reader.	Word choice includes various transition, descriptive and action words. Creates a clear picture for the reader.	Word choice is **adequate** because it adds only a bit of details. Uses familiar transition words. The reader begins to create a picture in their mind.	Word choice is **simple** and **repetitive**. Uses modelled transition words (e.g. Firstly, Secondly, Thirdly). The reader has a difficult time painting a picture in their mind.
Conventions	Mechanics are correct.	Paragraph has no punctuation, capitalization, grammar and spelling errors.	Paragraph has **very few** punctuation, capitalization, grammar and spelling errors.	Paragraph has **several** punctuation, capitalization, grammar and spelling errors.	Paragraph has **many** punctuation, capitalization, grammar and spelling errors.

2 of 2

For the downloadable rubrics or to modify it (e.g. change the criteria/levels) follow the link below.

Checklist - Kindergarten (teacher version)

Checklist - Kindergarten (student version)

Rubric - Elementary/Middle-School (teacher version)

Rubric - Elementary (student version)

Rubric - Middle-School (student version)

Rubric - Essay

https://forms.gle/5Ksoy3hVm5TZihxM8

About the Author

Nicole van Woudenberg is an award-winning teacher with over 25 years experience in education. Licensed in several jurisdictions, Nicole has worked at the elementary and high school levels in Ontario and Québec. She has held various leadership positions, including consultant, vice-principal and as Chair at the Ontario College of Teachers.

Nicole has served as a board member for several non-profit boards. Her knowledge in policy development and serving on various committees including finance, accreditation, legislation and quality assurance have contributed to positive changes and practices.

Over the span of her career she has authored, edited and published teacher guides, policy and procedure manuals, a newsletter serial as well as produced multi-faceted instructional videos for teacher-learning.

Her current project, the *85 After School* podcast, features retired teachers sharing their insights and passions post-teaching. Nicole continues to develop resources for educational practitioners which you can find through the *85 After School* media profiles.

www.ingramcontent.com/pod-product-compliance
Ingram Content Group UK Ltd.
Pitfield, Milton Keynes, MK11 3LW, UK
UKHW020423250726
13967UKWH00007B/2789